Don't Let My Name
SCARE YOU!

Exposé of An African Prince Born in America: Controversies Many May Wish I Had Not Shared.

ABDUL RAHMAN
&
FUMI HANCOCK

Bestselling Author, TEDx Talk Speaker, Indiefest Film Award Winner & Psychiatric Mental Health Dr. of Nurse Practice

This book, (part of a Trauma to Recovery™ series) paints a raw picturesque story of a young Nigerian, American born Prince, the multiple traumatic assaults on his sexuality, his struggles with "tabooed" mental illness, his impactful responses to the global pandemics plaguing America and the world at large, and candid advice to families whose lives are being shattered by poisons of secrecy.

His "Aunty," "Big Mummy, "is known globally as the Princess of Suburbia®, Over 16x Bestselling Author, TEDx Talk Speaker, Indiefest Film Award Winner & a Board Certified Psychiatric Mental Health Dr. of Nurse Practice, lending her own story of suicidal attempt and her literary platform to Abdul Rahman's Powerful story of healing, transformation, and daily transition from trauma to recovery.

This book, part autobiography, educational, inspirational, motivational, and an "an in your face" presentation is a "love letter" to all of the "Abdul Rahman" (who feels rejected, damaged, down-casted and out) in the world and their families who are trying desperately to understand how to help their loved one.

To families who seem like they have gotten is all wrong; to those who do not truly understand mental illness, here is your chance to look candidly through the eyes of Abdul Rahman and Dr. Princess Fumi Hancock!

It is time we begin to push this global pandemic into the front-line rather than the backdrop of other issues that have exploded on our medical platforms.

To our leaders who have taken their eyes off what's importance and are causing the deaths of many of our promising youths, it's time to get serious, and recognize the impact of our words. It's time to do right by them.

To our Christians who readily declare their conservative point of views yet ostracize those who do not look like them, talk like them, think like them, or perhaps are dealing with inner conflicts, will you do what JESUS would do?

To our Muslim brothers and sisters, this book will hopefully provide you the freedom to speak up, and not die in pain.

To my African brothers and sisters, secrecy has always been a part of our culture. While some success comes out of certain secrecy, the one we are talking about here is totally different. Stop the curse by telling the truth about your horrid past.

As for the pandemics which plague the world at large, it is time we begin to push this global pandemic (mental illness) into the front-lines rather than the backdrop of other issues that have exploded on our medical platforms.

What is Abdul Rahman's response to the current state of affairs in America, COVID19, Systemic Racism, and Mental Illness?

Are you looking for a book that will bring an eye-opening account and a visual representation of a mind trapped in schizoaffective disorder, bulimia, and other co-morbid disorders? THIS IS A MUST READ AND A MUST SHARE FOR YOU. It may very well save your loved one. Knowledge is power.

DEDICATION

To those who are suffering from mental illness across the globe; our vulnerable ones who reside in communities with silent cultures, either in America or other parts of the world, WE SALUTE YOU ALL. To those who have crossed our paths, to teach us lessons which are either good, bad, ugly or indifferent; we are whom we are today because of you... so here we go, YOU ARE FORGIVEN, YOU ARE RELEASED, and Abdul Rahman and I, Princess Fumi Hancock stand in our truth today, no matter how difficult this journey is about to get.

Telling the truth is not always easy, so we take this time to equally thank all of our family members who have given us the liberty to share without shame, guilt, or disgrace. We are proud of who we are regardless of the traumatic events which have laced the fabric of our being, but we rest in the solace that we come from the loins of those who are resilient, powerful, and have supported us to break the cycle of silence, and tell the truth despite ramifications. To our international and national communities who stand and fight for social justice, we thank you for reminding us that regardless of what position we are, TRUTH must prevail in the face of the pandemics we are facing: COVID19, Systemic Racism, and the incredible surge of Mental Illness ravaging our nation, America, and across the globe.

To All of my fearless millennials, Gen Z's, who have awoken the spirit of due diligence, thank you. Your heroic actions have given us wings to share our stories without blame or shame. To our loving immediate family members, we are eternally grateful for always standing by us and cheering us on, even when things are difficult and it seems, that we can no longer push on; YOU ALWAYS KNOW THE RIGHT WORDS TO SAY…. WE THANK YOU.

Keep the truth coming, it keeps us humble.

CONTENTS

DEDICATION vii

ACKNOWLEDGMENTS xi

PRELUDE to Don't Let My Name Scare You! 13

CHAPTER 1. MY NAME IS Abdul Rahman 19

CHAPTER 2. A Lighter Side of the Coin 29

CHAPTER 3. Another Moment the Earth Stood Still 39

CHAPTER 4. Dumping Religion for Spirituality 49

CHAPTER 5. I Cried! 59

CHAPTER 6. Life on the Edge 69

CHAPTER 7. I Will Not Shut My Eyes… 79

CHAPTER 8. The Poison of Secrecy 87

CHAPTER 9. COVID19 and the Other Pandemics 91

CONCLUSION 99

THE AUTHOR 103

THE CO-AUTHOR 105

What People Are Saying About Abdul Rahman 107

ACKNOWLEDGMENTS

First, we acknowledge GOD, the Almighty; the one who wakes us up daily; particularly in the chaotic climate we live in today.

We acknowledge the media reporters and correspondents, who risk their lives to ensure that we are as a nation know but more importantly, SEE the truth; you are all appreciated.

To all of the front-liners' to trauma, those who have been sexually molested, raped, shut down from telling their truth, parents who have buried their loved ones due to violence, our registered nurses, the advanced nurse practitioners, techs, physicians, fire-fighters, the military, navy, air-force, police officers (both active and retired), organizations dedicated to helping people suffering from mental illness ... many of you have truly dedicated their lives to serving our country, "experts and scientists," few elected government and political officials who have decided to say "ENOUGH IS ENOUGH", and others who are specifically not mentioned here, WE ARE THANKFUL FOR YOUR SERVICE and TOGETHER, Prince Abdul Rahman and Princess Fumi Hancock join in the solidarity.

PRELUDE *to* Don't Let My Name Scare You!

Until we all begin to stand for truth, justice, and we are able to look oppositions in the face then tell the truth, our world will never change.

Let me start off by saying this, I am Dr. Princess Fumi Hancock, an African Princess living in Diaspora, American Board Certified Psychiatric Mental Health Dr. of Nurse Practice, Bestselling Author, Johnsons & Johnson Nurse Innovator Fellow, often called the Princess of Suburbia® across the globe and **THIS IS ABDUL RAHMAN'S STORY!** His truth, discoveries and conclusions on what his life journey has been... period!

It is his journey! He is not being political, spiritual or whatever anyone thinks! This is a raw picturesque story of a young African, American born prince via way of his mother, Princess Mojisola Adetutu from the Adumori Nigerian Royal Household! She is my sister!

So, what then is our ask? That you read and deduce with an open mind, as we both understand that everyone's journey or conclusions may differ. While this may bring controversies, this is HIS controversial life story and until we all begin to stand for truth, justice and being able to look oppositions in the face and still tell the truth, our world will never change.

Let me say this, some of our family members are afraid for us! They are afraid that some radical organizations may choose to bounce on these stories and we may not be safe in sharing. They may misinterpret and draw unnecessary conclusion. Some from Africa may wonder why we have chosen to release such a book! Some of our family members went as far as stating that the world we live in now, in America is so volatile and we may experience backlash on the controversies, HIS discoveries, and conclusions. We are ready for the challenges… We are used to the challenges. We are okay with people saying otherwise but we are confident that many will be restored, healing will begin in families who choose to pull back the curtains of their lives so that transformation can take place. This is our only incentive in taking this difficult yet necessary journey. Let's be very clear… CONCLUSIONS SHARED in this book come strictly from our personal experiences.

Abdul Rahman is healing as he writes this story! This book is part of his healing, transformation and hopefully his contribution and his legacy in bringing restoration to our chaotic world!

* * * *

August 20, 2020, Abdul-Rahman my nephew reached out to me… big mama at 12 midnight. At first, I wondered what he was doing up at that time. So, I was reading through WhatsApp. "Big Mommy,' he writes, 'Can you tell me how you overcame your suicide attempts? How did you do it?'"

I was in bed, getting ready to sleep when I jumped up quickly as I read the message. "What do you mean Abdul Rahman? Why are you asking?" "I have read your story and watched where you shared how you were fed up and you drove straight to Verrazano Bridge in New York…. I remember hearing how you attempted to plunge your car down the bridge!"

I was speechless! Till date, I had written 24 books, 16 bestsellers, helped several new authors become #1 Amazon Bestselling Authors, travelled across the globe, sharing stories, from United Nations, to Washington, D.C., London, Paris, Africa, and across United States of America. Some of my stories had been made into award winning films. I had even won several film awards in Hollywood but frankly, I didn't think many of my family members really read in details what I was sharing. I was truly moved by his questions but equally concerned.

He finally shared with me that September was the anniversary month of one of his suicide attempts. He further explained that he was concerned about the month and worried that the feelings may come back again. He was worried about moving into the month of September. Until he asked, I had not thought about that. You see, I had tried to complete suicide well over 25 years ago. I had lost my home, businesses, kicked to the streets with two boys who were barely 4 and 2! I had given my all to a man who promised to love and cherish me! I was essentially dumped of love, and discarded like a rag even though I am a Nigerian princess! I was ashamed to go back to my family! I couldn't tell them that my marriage, the same one they went along with only because I told them I was in love, had failed! What is real about this situation is that, not until Abdul Rahman asked the big question that I realized my own anniversary too was September 1995.

I began to speak life into my nephew and rededicated myself to helping him overcome! The following week, we were live on Facebook, sharing his personal experiences about mental illness and sexual assault. All I could do was sit there in complete disbelief! All I could think is what would the rest of the family say about this revelation? Little did I know that this was just a piece of the iceberg!

Rahman and I began to share our experiences at 12 midnight. We talked about the power of telling our stories... I expanded on how sharing my life stories, even in the face of some backlash has truly brough healing to my life and more importantly, to my readers across the globe.

Rahman went on to say how his self-esteem has really been assaulted by all of his experiences in life. This was something I had sensed myself. So, I went into full mode of intervention, something I was already used to as a Psychiatric Mental Health Dr. of Nurse Practice with clinics in Arizona, USA. I knew it was time for him to share his story. It was time for him to join me on my podcast and my online TV broadcast, if he was ready. Rahman's face lit up! He was ready!

Only, I wasn't ready for what he was going to be sharing! With the first broadcast, it took everything in me to compose myself as he shared his mental health challenges as one who had been diagnosed with schizoaffective disorder, bipolar type; my head was set ablaze when he began to share the series of suicide attempts; his stories of certain pastors telling him he needed to pray more; of those who said it was his fault to have ended up with such diagnosis; the ignorant "so-called half illiterate who disguise in academia and spiritual heads" who told him he was only seeking attention! If it was not for grace...This young man went through all of these assaults and obstacles while trying to seek help... Today, I join him in sharing his story while I remind my readers of mine... I show and share a story of a gallant young

African-American born prince... my prince, Abdul-Rahman.

    We begin the journey.... *Come away with us....*

CHAPTER 1.
MY NAME IS Abdul Rahman

No, Nigeria is not a jungle.

My name is Abdul Rahman. *Don't let that scare you. My name means, "Servant of the Most Merciful."* I am proud to be living up to this name and I will not change it to make you comfortable. Yes, I have a long beard and I am growing my hair out but let me assure you, I am not a terrorist. As you will soon learn, I'm actually similar to some of you and in other ways, marvelously created. With hands raised, I surrender my story to you. My Father is my judge and has written over my life, everything you will now read.

I was born to Nigerian parents in Staten Island, New York; a borough that brought solace and gave refuge to many African migrants like my smooth face, beautifully fair, mother. My mom was alone in that cold hospital room in St Vincent's Medical Center; laboring for at least 16 hours. She was a young mother, inexperienced, blissfully naive, and innocent. While talking to my mom she recalled during her pregnancy with me that my biological father had impregnated three other women… *Really? What a con artist...* I thought. "I was lied to!" she exclaimed. I actually felt the anguish in her soft heart, evident in her breaking voice. The horrid nature of my deliverance would leave a gaping wound in that tender, secret place. I came out only by way of forceps. Forceps... It's believed that this is what left me with only one working eye. My birth could have never happened as only a few months prior, my mom survived a violent encounter with armed robbers on the highways of Nigeria.

No, Nigeria is not a jungle. I remember my classmates always asking me if I saw elephants and tigers. I can't say whether it was racist or just stupidity. We are far from poor. Nigeria is made up of beautiful cities and villages. One such city is Lagos where I'd spend most of my time whenever I would visit in my teenage years. The night life is lively! Workers of the Red-Light District parade the street in colorful and appealing high heels, miniskirts, and low-cut tops flaunting their God given assets. If that's your thing, go for it, you're in much luck. Our ladies are finer. Only kidding... Besides that, there's music everywhere. From the church to the marketplace. Shouting is not really shouting but an effort to get the other person to hear you. However beautiful Nigeria is, it is also very congested and chaotic. Two lanes of traffic can easily become five and no one is willing to let the other go in front of them. There was no way my mother could've been delivered out of their hands except by God. I remember her telling me, one of the attackers was going to kill her but the leader told him to spare her life. She was brutally hit with the end of the armed man's gun. Doctors who treated her following the assault, administered valium to my mother. My mother tells me now that she deeply regrets that, that had happened. No pregnant woman should receive valium as part of a treatment plan and likely contributed to my poor development growing up.

Let's talk about my father. Remember him? He's the man who impregnated three other women. My father is a prominent man in Nigeria, and he is known for his successful car dealing business. Everyone knows his name, which I will not mention here for his privacy. I respect his work ethics and have learned a great deal about the importance of money and being a faithful steward of it. Even with that, I have trouble saving money which I'll get to in another chapter. The world knows when he marries a new wife and they celebrate with him. It saddens me though that his love is not for one only but shared with multiple women. I cannot fathom that and don't want to understand. How special could my mother have been to him? In recent years, I've discovered that she, my siblings, and I were just a number. That realization fueled the rage I have towards my father. There were multiple times in the past few years where I swore to myself, I would not mourn if he died and I meant it. Only Satan's son could conjure up such vile hatred for a man who helped birth me; so, I must be. Ask me if I still feel that way and I would be rather slow and ashamed to tell you, "Yes, I despise him." Why should I hate the man who created me? I don't like him because simply put, he wasn't around most of my life. I reckon he was so quick in supporting and loving on all his other children but when it came to the children of his special wife, he could care less. That's okay because I don't need him as I once thought I did. What hurts more is that he hurt so many women in the same manner as he hurt my mother. It's so maddening to think that he used women like that and is okay with what he did. The amount of trauma he caused is unbearable to fathom. I say this as an empath and his son who is deeply grieved by his actions. In talking with my mother, I realized something though. I came to realize he may not actually know what he is doing. I recall many conversations my mother and I have had regarding my father's polygamous lifestyle and it hadn't occurred to me that he could actually be struggling with mental illness. My mother coined the idea to me. It's humbling to think about. Perhaps I shouldn't be so enraged at my father. He couldn't have known. But I'm inclined to believe he did know. Imagine every sweet word he said to each wife to be. It's sickening to think about and very devastating. It's devastating for me because I can't help but call this man my father as he helped create me and I'm devastated for every woman who crosses his path that he decides to marry.

After revealing what I had about my father, you might be thinking to yourself, *what was your childhood like?* This question is usually what Freudian psychologists or counselors would ask in a therapy session. You know, the therapy session where you're on a long couch, drifting off, trying to think of something to complain about. It's okay to ask. Keep in mind, not everyone with a dark past or childhood ends up developing mental illness. Also, not everyone who is mentally ill had a harrowing upbringing. That said, I'm one of those who did. I do not complain all that much about my childhood. That is partly because I feel judged as a victim and oft, I do not let myself express my pent-up grief even though I'd be justified. Let me be very clear with you, dear friend… I am not a victim, but I am a survivor. I will not deny the evil I have been handed by this life we all hold onto so swiftly, but I will not die. I refuse to.

It began when I was 7 years old. It was my birthday and I was in Nigeria at the time. I was in the family house that my father had constructed for all of his wives and his children. In our culture, the older sibling lays on the bottom bunk while the younger lays on the top. It's an honor and respect thing which some of my uncultured American friends may not understand. After this incident though, my family and I concurred that I should always sleep on the bottom bunk if I was in a similar situation. It was in the middle of the night and I had woken up. I was still groggy, and the bathroom door was inches away. The air was cold. I began my flight down the stairs on the side of the bed and I must've slipped or skipped a few steps I fell backwards onto a very hard floor. Needless to say, it was not good for me. I remember seeing blood when I tried to turn my head and I tasted it in my mouth. I passed out and woke up in the hospital. I had been covered with a white sheet as I was pronounced dead. I don't know for how long, but I remember my mom saying she prayed a prayer and I came to. I remember the moment I came out of death's grip and till this day I remember everything I saw on the other side. When I opened my eyes, my head hurt to move. I struggled to release myself from the numerous sheets I was put under. You hadn't seen a zombie until someone you love comes back from death. Imagine the look on my mother's face. I remember seeing my father standing by the window with a very neutral almost cold and indifferent look on his face and my mother was inconsolable. After I recovered, we lived in the family house/compound for a while and moved back to the United States.

Witchcraft is real.

What was it like in the family compound, you ask? There was a lot of mistrust, fear, spying, witchcraft, and the fear of it. I remember coming home one day after spending time with my half-brother. While I was with my half-brother, we had played video games and someone in the house asked if I wanted to eat rice and stew and I excitedly said yes. So, I had eaten the rice having forgotten that my mom told me never to eat anything from anyone. When realization of what I had just done came to me, my heart sank, and I began to fear. I went home and my mother beat me upon my confession. In hindsight, I understand why she did, and I respect that. It taught me a lot. You can't trust anyone especially in a polygamous household. I won't go into my mom's story as that is hers, to tell but witchcraft is real. I don't care what anyone says. I know it more than anyone how real it is. If I wanted to, I could get into the occult, but I know it won't be good for my mental health and my soul. Heck, I'm not trying to spend eternity with the spirit being that tried to kill me on numerous occasions just because he knew what I was going to do in this life. Being first born makes you a target. I was a target ever since I was born. When my mom presented me to my paternal grandmother, my mother recalls my grandmother taking me into a room and locking the door behind us. We were in there for a long while and till this day no one knows what happened in that room, but we suspect it wasn't good. As you'll find out later, I have been in sketchy, occultic situations even in my teenage years, while in Nigeria.

When I was 10 years old, my mother, my sister and I were living in the U.S. I was sexually assaulted. I can't say the "R word" as it's far too humiliating. What happened is far too traumatic to bear the full weight of, so I lessen it. I was violated to the point where I am plagued with flashbacks about the events of that day in our basement (where I currently sleep) and that brisk night at his house. I feel him all over again when I'm in a flashback. I literally feel him in my body.

Part of my childhood was watching my father pray. I was fascinated by it. My father never really pushed his children to conform to Islam, but he led by example. When my mother married him, she became a Muslim and was called Barakat meaning, "blessing." I recall my father praying one night, with his green mat below him and I bowed down with him. I didn't know what I was bowing to. I simply followed what he did. I loved "praying" with him. I followed him to mosque on Fridays. However, I was taken aback by the ritual of cleansing and the separation of men and women. I couldn't understand it. I had a thought in my mind. *You have to do all this to get to God?* After that experience, I resolved in my mind to be agnostic, dare I say atheist.

I had a personal vendetta against God and His people. I made fun of the people of God and became angry when someone would merely mention the name of God or Jesus of Nazareth. *Don't you dare mention His name around me. He f****d me over and did nothing to stop the abuse,* I thought. It took a long while for me to come around but even when I did, I had no idea what I was getting into. It wasn't until I was 17 years old that I discovered what it meant to be committed to Christ and His work. I was at Harvey Cedars Retreat with classmates of mine from a Christian school I went to at the time. While there, one of my classmates who I was in a gang with, exposed himself to me in front of one other gang member and a roommate of mine. I vividly remember the other gang member saying, "You traumatized him for life." He wouldn't be wrong in saying that. That said, I was aroused by the experience (after it had occurred mind you not during the experience). This would add to my sexual confusion which I will get into later. On the third and last day of the retreat, I was in the auditorium along with my other classmates and the pastor spoke on death. A holy fear and silence fell upon everyone there. After the message, during a moment of worship, I encountered the precious Holy Spirit. I fell immediately to my knees and I wept with a godly grief and in repentance for hours. The tears would not relent. I knew from that point onward that God was calling me to be separate from the crowd; especially the one I was hanging with. I found God but no one brought me to Him. He sought me out and I was in the right place at the right time. God knows when to show up.

While I was a Christian, I was and am by no means a sheltered kid. I've had many covertly and overtly sexual encounters with different boys/men in school. Besides the Harvey Cedar's incident, there was a moment when I was schooling in Nigeria and one of my classmates, sat on me and started molesting me violently while the whole class laughed. It was disturbing but pleasurable. I let the groping continue to happen and my classmate then asked if I was gay. Of course, I had to say no, right? Being gay could get you killed in Nigeria. For some reason I wanted to spare my life, but I was also deeply ashamed. In another instance, my classmate who was two years younger than me at the time, followed me into the bathroom. We used the urinal and my classmate stared intensely at me and then he inched closer to me after saying my genitalia was "So big." We play fought and he wanted to pee in my urinal with me and I was aroused. He smacked my behind and I followed suit and we held hands as we were leaving the bathroom. There was another time while I was in college where a man I went to English class with, caressed my back while I was in Chapel service and I let him because I froze. He told me in another situation, to come sit beside him and I did, and he pulled me towards him to lean on his shoulders. I was 10 years old again. It's sad to say but it felt right. I felt like I was with my abuser all over again and I was okay with that. All these experiences and many more have made me comfortable with the idea of me being with a man. These situations I've been in with my classmates have only further convinced me of what I may be.

Not only was I attracted to guys, I also thought I was a girl. All my dreams were emasculating and were grotesquely detailed. I recall one in particular where I had a period and I was wearing pink female underwear. This was the peak of my gender confusion and is partly why I keep a beard. I keep my beard, in part, to convince myself I'm really not a girl. But I'll be honest, I still feel like one. After all, *men don't get sexually assaulted. Only girls experience that*, I thought. Prior to these dreams and the confusion, I remember trying on my mom's earrings as a child, while in my mom's car. It soon became very apparent to me that boys do NOT wear earrings. "No, put that down!" My mother exclaimed. "That's for girls." I'm not gonna lie, I felt really guilty and slightly ashamed. I wanted to wear those earrings. When I put them on, it felt innate? I was at home in my body. My eyes lit up with fervor for freedom. My heart fluttered with excitement as I finally got to be curious, but it was not okay. That isn't the only time my girl side came out. When I was younger, I enjoyed my time with dolls. I was not like your typical little boy who played rough and drooled over cars and action figures. No… I was damn sensitive. A "p****" like my classmates called me. I liked my barbies (which I stole from my sister. Sorry, haha) and I cried at sappy things like my aunt getting married. My classmates knew I was different, and they marked me quickly and without reserve or mercy. QUEER. Even now, it's ringing so loudly in my head. I was queer, they concluded.

CHAPTER 2.
A Lighter Side of the Coin

On a much lighter note, I want you to get to know a different side of me that is not so dark. I love music! I credit by brother, Abdul Razaaq II (meaning, Servant of God, the Provider) for helping me fall in love with music! My love for music partly stemmed from my jealousy of his remarkable talent. I was mesmerized as I heard his music lessons from a far. I'd do anything to be in the room with him and sit at the feet of greatness. The sound that came from his keyboard was enchanting ... incredibly captivating. I had to have a piece of that gift. One day, I had the chance to sit in on Razaaq's piano lesson. It was nearing the end of the lesson and he got to preform for us. He played *Ode to Joy* which is one of my favorite Christmas themed hymns or carols and has since become one of my mom's favorite piano songs that I play often. It was amazing to be under the influence of music. I was not short of tears as I basked in the beauty of the precious moment. I knew within my heart that I had to start playing piano. I begged my mom for maybe a few good months, but her response was a big no. I understand this because paying for two children's lessons would be a lot. So, I held my peace as I attended all his performances. *Maybe some of his magic will rub off on me.* I remember seeing him in a formal white shirt and he shone like the sun. He took position left stage and began to play his song numbers. I could've sworn something else entered the space we were in. Not even the flies from the humid outdoors could interrupt the glory that fell on all of us present. If this was heaven, I wanted to stay here forever. He finished playing his songs and he took a bow. I knew in that moment that I wanted to be a performer. It was a big dream for someone who's never touched an instrument before, but I had to tap into what my brother had and quick. I recall congratulating him with joy in my heart but like I said earlier, I was jealous. I coveted so hard after this anointing he had.

Meanwhile back at home, I remember trying to find the keyboard. *Where could they have hidden it?* I thought. When I did find it, I couldn't find the plug needed to play it. I was infuriated that I couldn't mirror the sound I've heard from Razaaq's fingers. One fateful day, the keyboard had been moved to the living room and the plug was in place. Finally, I had the opportunity to play music. My heart began to race, and my eyes became blurry as I inched towards the keyboard. Just brushing my fingers against the keys, made me tear up. I made sure no one was looking. This was my special encounter with my love. I turned on the keyboard and pressed a key and the world suddenly revolved around me. I felt eyes on me, and I became uneasy because I had thoughts that I shouldn't be touching this expensive instrument. Nevertheless, I began to play Für Elise after only hearing it once in my life. I played it from memory. Out of nowhere, my mom came near by me and stood in shock, letting out gasps. I was the star of the show now. She asked me how I learned to play, and my natural response was, "I don't know," I said shrugging my shoulders and wearing a small grin. As much as I enjoyed being in the spotlight for a little while, it's usually hard to accept compliments from others. Fast forward to today, I compose music on my free time and record my pieces for my own enjoyment but I'm looking forward to making an album. I ran to tell Mack of the experience I just had!

Mack was a gorgeous black and tan/cream German Shepherd. He was my loyal and sweet best friend. I remember the day we welcomed him into our family. My lovely sister named Zainab, (which means Fragrant Flower) had been begging my mom for a dog for years. I mean begging! My sister and I would kneel at the feet of my mom and sing the song we sing till this very day, "Please mommy please, please mommy please, please mommy please... Can we (fill in the blank with whatever a child would want to do)?" Her answer was almost always no. Especially when it came to a puppy and she never explained why. Not even our puppy dog face could change her mind. But she compromised in some instances on the condition that we finish our chores or do our homework.

As far as pets go, my mom was kind enough to give my sister a hamster. Zainab's experience with our first pet was not a pleasant one. Tina was a black hamster and her eyes were as black as midnight on solstice in December. I remember the moment my sister reached into her cage as she usually does. I'm sure she'll never forget it. Needless to say, there was a lot of blood and endless tears. It really hurt me when I saw Zainab cry and to watch her experience, the unfathomable pain. Tina was her beloved and Zainab was only trying to clean her cage. Imagine the betrayal she felt in that moment. She ran inside and ran water over her finger, all while crying. Who would blame her? I sure didn't. I was angry at Tina funnily enough. I didn't want her anymore since she was a big meanie.

Let's fast forward to the day Mack became a part of our lives. My mom came home in her light gold Nissan Murano. As soon as she parked, she called my sister to come and open the door. I was standing by the stairs which

31

led to the entrance of the house. As my sister opened the door, my heart began pounding as I didn't know what to expect. All of a sudden, my sister let out a scream I'd never heard before and till this day. My eyes were wide open as out came Mack; beautiful German Shepherd puppy. My sister's eyes welled up with happy tears. I've never seen her so ecstatic in my life. "Thank you, mommy! Thank you!" she exclaimed bowing in reverence to my mother (It's in our Nigerian culture to kneel down or prostrate to our elders when they give us a good thing like money or when you give them something like food and argh yes, when you wake up in the morning). Even I started to well with tears. I couldn't show it though. It was Zainab's moment! In the days that followed, my mom made it clear to us the commitment that it was to have a dog and my sister seemed ready for the task. However, frustrating it might've been to brush his teeth or wash him, she did so with humility and love because she adored Mack. I loved Mack also; even though it was my sister who did the hygiene aspect of taking care of him. I loved giving him food from whatever we got from Tantalizers or Mr. Biggs, popular restaurants in Nigeria. Besides feeding him, Mack and I had conversations outside the house. The conversations were one sided obviously but I know he heard me loud and clear. I remember telling him about feelings of depression and loneliness that I was having and how I wasn't doing well in school and my father's response to that. His presence was so calming. I didn't feel judged or misunderstood. We had to keep Mack outside as in Islam, a dog is an unclean animal and cannot be inside the house under any circumstances. It even prevents the angel of mercy from entering the home. Mack was a quiet dog but very playful. I remember him licking me non-stop on the face and pinning me with his paws. It was such a special bond we had. I remember touching his nose and he'd show his teeth; very beautiful, sharp teeth. It didn't scare me though as he wasn't a violent dog towards me or any of my siblings. After he would show his teeth, he'd go back to licking me. I miss him so much! Upon leaving Nigeria to head back to the United States, Mack had to be placed with someone else. Till this day, I have no clue what happened to him. We can only assume he's now dead as a result of not being cared for. We heard reports that he became aggressive all of a sudden and the person we gave Mack to, didn't want him anymore but it was too late to change the deal. It hurts not having him here with me but I'm blessed whenever I see a German Shepherd resembling our Mack! Depression is incredibly difficult to handle without an animal of some kind. They are gifts to humanity and still some treat them so poorly.

Let's talk more about Zainab (Z for short). I love Zainab. I really do. I think it shows in many instances where she was sick or hurt in some way. I would cry for her. Like this one time where she bumped her head on the counter in a store and she said she was seeing stars. I was eating a sandwich but I had lost my appetite and was crying heavily after I heard that as I was filled with terror. My mom said that it was okay and that I should eat my sandwich. No wonder food is such a comfort to me even now. I didn't want anything bad to happen to Zainab and I couldn't control that so I sniffled and swallowed my tears with food. Perhaps I'm just very empathic as others have noted about me. That said, I also felt a sense of duty to protect and watch over Zainab to make sure she was okay at all times. My mom recalls me sharing my piece of chicken with her without even hesitating. I would do anything to make anyone feel happy or comfortable, especially my sister. There were also so many times where I was so proud to call her my sister! For instance, in Planet Hollywood, someone stuck her tongue out at Zainab and Zainab being the feisty Gemini that she is after a while of putting up with it, stuck her tongue out back at the girl. I think the girl ended up crying. In my head, I was like, "YAS, you go girl!" Zainab was that girl and is now that woman who is always there for her friends and people she loves dearly. I can't lie, she would get on my nerves when I wanted to do something bad to myself and she would be home in the nick of time to catch me in the act or ask me what my plan was. Who could forget those times when she would sing loudly on road trips I was forced to go on? But all in all, she's an amazing person who deserves credit for putting up with all my bull crap.

Just to drive home the idea that she's a kind and amazing person, I'll take you to when I was helping my sister move into her new studio. While she was unpacking, she brought out a knife and I didn't quickly realize it was mine. When I did, I was like, "That's my knife." She reminded me of a time when I gave it to her while I was struggling with cutting. I was shocked to find out that she had kept it. I figured she would just throw it out. She told me that I wouldn't get it back until I feel like I'm ready and we both laughed when she said that. We both know I'm not ready. She is so caring. That's why I felt very sad when she was leaving as I thought I had no one to protect me from myself. In talking with her, my therapist and my mom, I realized that God has been the one protecting me all this while and my sister is her own, beautiful person and deserves to live a life that is right for her.

Motherhood cannot be bought outright, neither can it be leased. You either have a true character of a genuine mother or you don't! The good news is that it is also a learned behavior as well as innate.

Remember the beautifully, fair, innocent woman I talked about in Chapter 1? She's my mother. My siblings and I affectionately call her Mommy. I don't think that will ever change. Call me a mama's boy but she's very special to me. I recall when I was in P.S. 54, there was a dance and I had become the dance king. "My queen" didn't want me to be king and she reluctantly gave me a crown and rolled her eyes at me. I'll never forget it. Then it was time for the mother and son dance. I danced with my mother and it was a powerful bonding moment. Then for whatever reason, I began to dance with her friend who was also a mother. We danced for a long while and I was looking for my own mom and when I found her, the first thing she said was, "you cheated on me!" My heart welled up with sorrow, guilt, and shame. I didn't mean to make her feel that way. She told me she was only joking but to me, it wasn't a joke. It was so serious to me that I remember apologizing all night and the day or two after. That's how special she is to me. She has endured a lot with me and has seen things no man or woman should see. I know the situations I've been in, in life has caused her much grief but despite all of that, Father's love permeates through her being and she holds no grudge unlike myself. She is a true daughter of the Most High. She always seeks to please Him and do according to His statutes by the power of the Holy Spirit.

I was heavily bulimic for 6 years in my early to mid-20s. For 4 of those years, my mom knew nothing about it. I was away at college a majority of the time. Before I was bulimic, I binge ate and didn't purge for a long time and I gained a bunch of weight which my mom saw and was deeply concerned by. I weighed in at 300+lbs. I ended up in a hospital near my college after suffering from what doctors called a brain aneurysm. My blood pressure was so high upon admission and I lost my ability to speak for about an hour. Soon after that experience, I discovered how to purge. My weight began to drop rapidly. People began to inquire of me, what I was doing to look so good. I had lost 70lbs at that point. I obviously couldn't tell them what I was doing so I lied and said, "Oh, you know. Just eating right and exercising…" No one had a clue I was suffering so badly with Bulimia. While I was on break from college, I would purge in the sink in the bathroom of our house. My mom confronted me one day and asked me why there was food in the sink. I told her I didn't know but I'm sure she knew that I knew. She locked the door of that bathroom. This would only be the beginning of trauma for my mother when it came to the eating disorder. At the peak of the bulimia, I was at 183 lbs. and was purging 4-5 times a day in garbage bags which I hid in the closet in my room. While I was not underweight, I was still in pain, like some of you reading. I hid the disorder well until I couldn't hide it anymore. One day, my mom had come into my room at random and decided that we needed to clean. I was terrified because I knew what was in my room and didn't want anyone to see that. I remember the moment I came downstairs after she had discovered my puke bags. It wasn't until my mom carried a leaking bag of my vomit, that I realized I was sick, really sick. Her response was only natural. I broke her heart that day. Watching her collapse to the floor asking God what she had done to deserve this, only intensified the hatred I had towards myself. It really wasn't about her but the Bulimia doesn't just affect me, it affects everyone around me. *This is one more person that I hurt. I'm a monster.* My mother's words confirmed it to me. I was "wicked…" I wanted to console her but I was too ashamed to speak and didn't want to make her even more upset. The bulk of the next two years was filled with fear, mistrust, and lying (on my part).

I'd spend copious amounts of money on food in one day. All those "save your money" talks meant nothing to me. I was out of control. It got to the point where my mom had to monitor my bank account. She would do so at random. My heart would race as she asked me to go to my bank's website and go to my account. I would stall and try to convince her not to check my account. I was afraid but mainly ashamed of everything I did with that money. All of my money was spent on food. Food I did not need. There was food at home. What the hell was I doing? I couldn't stop. After a while, my mom stopped asking to see my account and would instead ask me, "You're not spending your money, are you?" and I would say no. Treatment was not and is not an option for me. I owe thousands of dollars just for receiving mental health treatment that was not eating disorder specific. My mom makes it a point to tell me how much debt is on her head because of me. I obviously can't pay it as I have no income, so I feel guilt. Not everyone can afford quality ED treatment. So, it begs the question, is recovery for me? My mother is so strong for seeing me through the thick of the misery I was enduring and not giving up on me.

CHAPTER 3.
Another Moment the Earth Stood Still

This is not about ME but about ABDUL RAHMAN and every other voiceless ABDUL RAHMAN out there, be it in America or any parts of the world.

Wat do you do when your nephew comes to you with so many big secrets... the thoughts in his head, some clear, others which could be construed as borderline fantasy, yet you know this is his truth? As an avid reader, if you picked up this book, it is hopefully because you want to learn one or two things about life. Perhaps you are struggling with what my nephew is too; perhaps you have a niece or a loved one who has mental illness and what if it was you but you are unable to share with anyone the war you are experiencing inside of you?

Having survived the first chapter, it is my hope that the second chapter is light enough to give you that breather you need. I thank you for hanging in there. I thank you for not judging him or anyone else who may be going through this.

Many may wonder, Princess Fumi, why are you choosing to take this route to help your nephew? Why are you using this opportunity to share such explosive information? The truth be told, the world we live in today is completely different. Particularly in America where everything has turned upside down. America is in deep crisis and depending on who you are talking to, some will tell you she is eroding away; others will tell you there is still hope for a turn around and then, there are the few, hopefully, who are living in what I call the *lah-lah* land, who simply are not seeing the suffering of others.

In the midst of our crises, COVID19 pandemic and systemic racism, sadly, there is yet another up roaring, which is the mental health crisis. I watch as few media outlets do a "hit and run" with it. Some leaders even use it as a crutch for making a case why America should open up soon, yet they refuse to showcase their defiance against the scientist's predictions and course towards recovery. They encourage others by letting them believe that they are safe without following the CDC guidelines. They are leaders, more like masquerades parading as leaders (another topic for another book), pruning away at the hearts of Americans, flat-out lying, pretending to be one thing while we all know and can see they are another. People are being used as political pawns and yet they are okay with it.

Why am I sharing this, I am standing with my nephew in this because there will be backlash, we are expecting that. It is important for him to share his truth as we know there are many who will be reading this and are in the same boat like he is.

Many who know my stand as a born-again Christian may be confused about what I am getting ready to share in this chapter. Let me make this clear, I AM NOT CONFUSED. I have simply learned to offer compassion which I was not given at some point in my life. I therefore ask that I not be judged but that you will take me out of the equation and simply read and ponder on what I have to offer.

As a Board Certified Psychiatric Mental Health Dr. of Nurse Practice, I cannot tell you enough the number of patients I see from teenagers to teachers, therapists, psychologists, clergies, people in the government who are conflicted. Those who were already suffering with mental illness; those who dared not share their stories because they are men who have been molested, raped, tortured, bullied by powerful people. I have watched as patients walk into my clinic at 21 yrs. of age stating they are ready to be placed on medication and that if it is not done, they are afraid they will end up in jail for killing someone or they will be dead themselves. Our prison system is packed with men and women who are there today because they did not get the help they needed when they were younger. People did not believe them when they cried out in their own way that they were in crisis. As a society, we are eager to crucify, lynch, or whatever word you want to use, whoever does not fall int the box we have created in our heads.

The truth be told, regardless of what we may believe, PEOPLES' LIVES Matter, male, female, colored, transgender, gay...WE MATTER IN THE EYES OF OUR CREATOR, in spite of their sexual orientation, their religious believes.

My chapters in this book is not about my religious believes or background. It is not about how I was raised in Africa; it is not about ME but about ABDUL RAHMAN and every other voiceless ABDUL RAHMAN out there, be it in America or any parts of the world where we know that this book will reach.

Genuine Healing Begins When We Allow People to Share their Truths. It's about who is wrong but simply caring enough to FIRST LISTEN!

To the potential nay-sayers, to those who are prone to simply seeing their own views alone and not yielding to others', I say lend me your ears. You may have an Abdul Rahman in your home, who may be at the brink of taking his own life! *One Event Can Change Your Life Forever™!*

A while back, on one of the social medic platforms, I watched a short video which was put out by one of the leading catholic priests. He shared his views about abortion, his views of same sex marriages and how GOD was against it all. He expressed his opinion why one of our leaders whom *people believe* is in support of priests (and other conservatives) should be the one to lead America, though his life as a whole does not mirror this; he encouraged people to simply ignore every other blunder that person continues to commit unapologetically but that we need to be single-minded about our decision-making process in American politics. The truth be told, as a holy ghost tongue speaking Christian who was also raised in catholic schools, I understood where he was coming from. I have my own thoughts and ideas about this.

As a clinician, I have gotten to see and study more but more importantly spent time with a person who was raped by her uncle, got pregnant by her uncle; shamed out of a whole country and would rather die than keep that pregnancy! I have treated many who are at the throes of gender and sexual orientation discourse, as such, they have been castrated by my fellow Christians who were supposed to guide them gently. I continue to treat patients who have been raped mercilessly within the confinement of the church and was bullied, threatened that if they told, they were going to die and so were their family members! So, they resulted to hanging themselves! Like my nephew shared, some of my patients are not given the chance to even get to understand what they are feeling. The society they live in, once they think they figure them out, they guilt them and turn them instantly into beasts that cannot be amongst human beings. We literally make it difficult for that one who has found herself with the most difficult pregnancy to carry… that of her blood brother, that of her blood father… that of her uncle, to make decisions which matter to her life. We leave them to bear the cross yet we want to dictate everything else about their lives. We do not provide viable solutions and alternatives but are ready to condemn and cast the first stones.

Our world is changing and it is important how we address all of these issues without sending more people to resort to suicide as the only alternative.

A little over a year ago, I introduced to the world, a group of *Fearless Visionaries* who on my platform shared their stories or resiliency. From a young child who was kidnapped and thrown into a sack of rice and later found herself in America, to a now Engineer who was gang raped by 8 men, to a teenager who was abused by her then boyfriend and finding herself facing a gun to her face, to a Christian family who later found out that one of their children at considered suicide and the list goes on. You are welcome to check the book and these powerful stories out: Fearless Visionaries: TEAR THE VEIL™ (http://www.fearlessvisionaries.com/). It is truly an honor to continue to live life with these powerful women who last year we travelled the work together, sharing our stories. If we truly desire to create a world that's inclusive, then we must lay aside our own believes and thoughts; then begin to consider that of our neighbors', understand their plight, their struggles and start with the word *LOVE,* a word is quickly eroding away in today's America and the world as a whole. Let me interject here, that LOVE does not preclude sharing the truth in firmness. It simply means giving that person a chance to hear you without feeling judged. I believe in the word of GOD. I live my life with the principles laid therein and they have never failed me. ABDUL RAHMAN is a Christian too and I see my nephew, how he pushes to live a God-fearing life. I also believe in God's Grace and Mercy, without which none of us will exist today.

The Grace and Mercy We Have Been Freely Given by Our Creator; We Are Called Upon to Do the Same. It will require you laying aside your Judgement and Truly Embodying Our Creator's Selfless Character.

When my nephew told me that he had reached out to a pastor in his church about his mental illness and what he was feeling conflicted about (his sexual orientation) … the response he got was somewhat like this, *brother, you need to pray more. You are not praying like you should.* Not once did he ask, how are you doing, how are you coping, how can I help you? Rather, this pastor went into a full-blown attack on my nephew's personality. Our dear pastor felt my nephew must have been doing a lot of wrong things … perhaps this was God's way of punishing him.

What if he had just listened to him without judgement? What if he had first started by apologizing on behalf of the one who molested him in his pre-teens? What if he had helped him to understand why at a *Christian College Campus,* where he was sent because his mother felt he would be safe there, was worse than the outside world? The perversion that wreaked the campus, a Christian campus in the East Coast of America, was simply atrocious. What if our pastors begin to address those incidences which have exposed our sons, nephews and daughters to assault at their tender age? What if we exercised compassion, tempered with justice? What if despite our own Christian or Islamic beliefs, we made our leaders accountable for the atrocities they commit against humanity rather than pay people off, using church funds and wish them away? The *What ifs* are what I present in this chapter. A loved one once told me that I may never be able to change everybody's minds on these issues, but I will most certainly try to reach one. There is power in one.

What is my overall message here? It is that we as global citizens need to get our compassion back. We need to call to order those things which are already misaligned at the beginning, before we can begin to solve problems at the surface level. We must understand that love, though sometimes firm, will go a long way towards helping others than bullying them into submission. We must be very careful to put ourselves in the shoes of others before we proceed to dictate how they should live their lives.

"Why do you look at the speck of sawdust in your brother's eye and pay no attention to the plank in your own eye? [4] How can you say to your brother, 'Let me take the speck out of your eye,' when all the time there is a plank in your own eye? [5] You hypocrite, first take the plank out of your own eye, and then you will see clearly to remove the speck from your brother's eye." – Matthew 7:3-5

While I may not agree with your stance on your sexuality, I can show you love, I can walk alongside YOU, I can empower you, I can help you, I can be there for you, I can hope the best for you, I can restrain from making you feel like a demon or a beast, I can make sure that you do not feel worse than you already do... I can SIMPLY BE QUIET and JUST LISTEN. Because I love you and care deeply for you, I can stand in prayer with you and for you. I can lend a helping hand., helping you to see all options (if there are options to whatever issues you are struggling with) so that you can make the right decision for YOU.

In the bible, Jesus preached and then retreated. Every time He would teach, He would retreat and allowed his disciples to make decisions. He was there for you but He allowed them and encouraged them to make their decisions. In fact, at some point, when there was a heavy storm and they were in a boat... everything rocking around them. In fear, they went to Him who was sleeping through the storm. He instantly calmed the storm on their behalf and commanded it to be still and it was still! Then, He turned to them to teach them why it is important that they learned to fly on their own (Matthew 8:23-27 KJV). This is a great example of what He did throughout the bible. True leaders do not incite chaos, neither do they cause division. They calm the storm. Calming the storm starts with starting with what must all agree on... *THAT ALL MEN/ WOMEN WERE CREATED EQUAL.* For those of my Christian brothers and sisters, who are familiar with Genesis, it reads: *In the Beginning, GOD created the heavens and the earth and ALL that dwelleth therein* (Genesis 1 KJV) .... *So, God created man in his own image, in the image of GOD created he him, **male and female** create he them.* Genesis 1: 27KJV. And when he saw All that He had created, He thought them ALL good, and on the seventh day, He rested.

Jesus would share life parables, He would heal, and then teach - empowering them to begin exercising their own individual spiritual powers. Is this what we are practicing? Many times, what I have observed is us having an opinion about everything without even trying to find out how the party involved is thinking or feeling. We make judgement calls on people we have never met, experiences we have never had, places we have never been, and we call our own judgements *the gospel.*

If we are going to change the world for the better, so that generations behind us are left with the same compassion we were afforded, we must begin to let down our guards; we must allow peace to reign, we must remember that we are all living under grace and mercy; above all, we must refrain from throwing stones at other peoples' houses when we in turn live in a glass house.

CHAPTER 4.
Dumping Religion for Spirituality

I don't believe in rituals to cast out a supposed demon of binging and purging or Major Depression, when it's clearly a mental health issue that needs medical intervention.

I'm not a fan of religion. I'm all for faith or spirituality and expressing that freely but what religion makes people do is sickening and pisses me off, quite frankly. I am not religious, and I will shout it loudly if I had the voice to do so. I shared my conversion experience earlier in this book and you might be wondering why I'd make such a bold statement so as to almost renounce my faith in Jesus, the Christ. There is a difference between being religious and being a Christ follower. It's no fault of your own if you believe the two to be synonymous with one another. You hear a lot about or see religious people in the media. Whether that's in cartoons like The Simpsons (one of my favorite shows), South Park, or on the news when a religious group of people decide to do something so degenerate that it warrants a story. For example, the Westboro Baptist Church. I'm sure you're familiar with them. You know, the people who held signs that read "God hates fags." They are also the same people who protested at the funerals of military soldiers holding signs that thanked God for 9/11. It's gross to think on. People like the Westboro Baptist church exist in every denomination of Christianity. From Lutheran to Pentecostal. It should also be noted that having the title Muslim or Christian, isn't enough. It doesn't make you a noble person. What's in your heart will come out through your actions and your words. The people you see on the news or portrayed in comedic television are not true Christians or Muslims. They are simply bigoted, misinformed, leeches who sneak into our houses of worship and take away our purity by sowing partiality and discord among the brethren and those who come as seekers. So, what makes Christ followers different from religious people? The element of compassion is missing in the religious. True religion is caring for the orphans, the widows, the needy and those in bonds; which includes those battling mental illness. The outliers are often left out or ignored because the religious aren't equipped to deal with what isn't the norm. They aren't comfortable with sitting with the needy and broken as they have forgotten where they've come from. There are still some who thank God for not being like their neighbor who drinks heavily, or they thank God for not being gay; because the straight guy isn't going to burn in fire and be reviled and punished in unfathomable ways by demons forever and ever right? It's only those who are gay... The religious tend to look down on these precious souls. They forget the parable Jesus told concerning two groups of people who stood before the Son of Man. Both groups of people were being judged. The Son of Man spoke to one group saying, "I was hungry and you fed me. I was naked and you clothed me. I was in prison and you visited me...What you do to the least of these, you do to me." Matthew 25: 35-40.

Compassion is the greatest form of love humans have to offer.
- Rachel Scott

Someone I feel deeply connected with on a spiritual level is Rachel Scott. Rachel was 17 years old when she was killed by two emotionally hurt men, Eric Harris and Dylan Klebold, on April 20th, 1999, while eating lunch with her friend. She had this theory that "If one person can go out of their way to show compassion, then it will start a chain reaction of the same." In her journal, she went on to say, "You never know how far a little kindness can go." I am inclined to agree with her when she says, "Compassion is the greatest form of love humans have to offer." If Jesus of Nazareth was moved with compassion even to his point that He healed the people, why aren't we showing compassion more? He is our standard. Jesus warned us that love will grow cold in these last days. Christians, we are not in war with the LGBTQ+ community or those who follow the tenants of true Islam. We are all brothers and sisters and made beautifully by our majestic Creator.

I've had my fair share of experiences with religious people. They were my friends and were part of churches I attended and one I am currently a member of. I've been the subject of many exorcisms on my college campus and at home. Yes, you read that right. I believe in God's power to heal and deliver but I don't believe in rituals to cast out a supposed demon of binging and purging or Major Depression, when it's clearly a mental health issue that needs medical intervention. I'd venture to say that some of what you call demon manifestation is actually hysteria brought on by anticipation that something would happen or belief that it is a spiritual issue. Not everything is a demon. I repeat, not every mental health or physical ailment is as a result of a demonic force. Demons are very real, might I add. Please, don't get me wrong. I of all people would know how real demons are. I'm simply bringing light to an issue that charismatic churches especially, refuse to address. We need to stop demonizing what makes us human. Not everyone struggles with mental illness but those who do are simply human and not vessels for jinn that we need to cast out all the time because we don't want to sit with the weight of the pain our loved ones are in. I was discouraged from seeking medical intervention for a long while and was told to seek God's face and pray more or for once. The thing about mental illness is, it affects every area of your life. From finances to your spiritual life. Praying was incredibly difficult. Let alone, reading the bible. It really discouraged me from going to God since I wasn't like other perfect Christians who also weren't mentally ill. I felt alienated and deserted by God because of the people He allows to be in His church. Hear me out, I understand well that Christians are humans. By no means am I perfect and never will be on this side of Heaven. Everyone puts up a good front. If we were only honest with each other, for crying out loud!

Fear makes you say hurtful things. So, from here onward, unless your words are full of grace, just don't say anything, please!

Where are the suicidal Christians who doubt God's existence? Where are the closet drug addicts? Where's the lusting Christian wife? We need to see realness in the church. I'm sick of the damn façade. Whenever I showed my dark side, the leaders and congregants were always so uncomfortable, and some said really hurtful things. In one instance, I was at a party with a group of people from church and one of them said, after talking about my crisis counselor experience, "How are you not depressed doing that kind of job?" I responded by saying, "I'm already depressed." One of the girls there began to laugh nervously almost to say, "we don't talk about that here." The woman who asked the question, said to me, "you have a good sense of humor." What's funny was, I wasn't even laughing. I was dead serious and being vulnerable was hard, but I felt like I could trust them. That was mistake #400. The rule is, when you're talking with so called Christians, don't talk about tattoos, homosexual feelings, and definitely don't talk about your mental health. When I was talking to an associate pastor of that same church, I'm a member of till this day, 2 years prior to the party, I mentioned my struggle with Bulimia and suicidal thoughts. Would you believe that one of the first things he said in response to my confession was, "God's judgment is on you..." As if that wasn't enough, he proceeded to say that God was teaching me a lesson for something I apparently did wrong. He also harshly said that he didn't understand why I would do something so gross. Every part of me died when he said that to me. Maybe it was my reaction to the truth, some of you might be thinking. Granted, the truth is a hard pill to swallow but it wasn't truth. He was spewing venom of disgust that I already had for myself and a hate for or ungodly fear of God. We shouldn't be so quick to attribute the pain of our brother or sister to a higher power. Sometimes life is rough and may appear to be running against to us and for no good reason. So, don't say there's a reason for everything. Not only do you not know that, but you forget that we may never find out that supposed reason on earth thus we have no closure. Maybe when we stop thinking that God is testing us or doing us bad, we'll stop asking "why?"

That pastor reminds me of Job's (Bible KJV, Job 4:23) friends who began to accuse him and repeatedly tell him that he must've sinned to have God punish him that badly. They should've stayed silent like they did for 7 days prior to their disgusting response to Job's cry. Maybe some of you are Job's friends. You are so quick to blame your oppressed friend for all the hell they've gone through in their life and their current nightmare they are enduring. Instead of sitting with them and acknowledging that you don't understand and showing grace, you act as though you know what would fix them or what the root cause of their issue is. Maybe you're a mother and you're distraught over the horrid thoughts of your young adult son or daughter and in anger or frustration over the helplessness you feel, you say, "You're seeking attention..." I've heard variations of this from people like, my mother (whom I love very much and who loves me too), the dean of the college I was kicked out of, and so-called friends. Even a registered nurse, from that same college, told me this after one of my suicide attempts. You'd think a nurse would have enough book knowledge to know not to say that to someone who just attempted suicide. These are professing Christians who told me this. Fear makes you say hurtful things. So, from here onward, unless your words are full of grace, just don't say anything, please. When I told my mom about a suicide attempt, she said I should stop seeking attention. Who would attempt suicide just so people can pay attention to them? I did not call her when I attempted to end my life multiple times nor will I ever call anyone if I really wanted to die. I simply wanted support or understanding. I couldn't get it at the time because she was afraid and didn't understand.

Get to know someone's story or struggle before you yell at them or use damning scriptures, especially over text.

I remember when I was 14 years old, my mom and I visited a psychologist who diagnosed me with severe depression. I recall his words so vividly, "You're sick…You need help. We can help you." Till this day I've never heard anyone put it so bluntly to me. That bald headed, gray suited, glass faced, African American psychologist was telling the truth. I kept denying the seriousness of it throughout the meeting, all the while looking at my mom. I couldn't be honest then. Not in front of her. Upon leaving his office, my mom and I sat in the car in silence for a while and she offered to get me the treatment I needed but I knew it was half-hearted as I knew she didn't believe in it at the time. So, I did what I do best. I lied and said that I was "fine" and that "everything will be fine." After which she said amen. Internally, I shook my head. I regret that moment. My heart sank as we pulled out of that parking lot. There was my chance to get better and I only got worse from that point on. I can't blame her though. Who wouldn't want their child to be fine? No mother prays concerning their child, "God, I hope my child is mentally ill so I can fear for him or her, lose precious sleep, and look after them constantly."

In response to my gender confusion, one of my "Christian" friends said, "STOP LETTING THE DEVIL CONFUSE YOU. YOU'RE NOT A GIRL!" As if that would change my mind. What hurt most is that he didn't even explore the reasons why I felt this way. He didn't even ask why I felt the way I felt. He was very invalidating. Get to know someone's story or struggle before you yell at them or use damning scriptures, especially over text. Now is not the time to argue with your brother or your sister in faith and attempt to win them over to your position that is likely not from holy scripture and is actually from your own bias. To be a +Christian is to be led by compassion. We are not to be led by pity or frustration. They will lead us to make horrible decisions.

I'm so grateful that my sweet, spiritually sensitive aunt is not religious. Being a Christ follower does not mean you do not disagree. You can and are free to do so. Even the religious disagree and it is their right. It's the way they go about it. They hurt people rather than heal. My beliefs are not liberal or conservative. There's no need for dumb labels or division. Christ isn't about that. My beliefs are uniquely mine that I've come to hold true through personal experience which some of you reading may have lived in a similar way. My beliefs about sexuality, tattoos, and mental health are very unpopular among my fellow Christians. I'm unconventional and happy to be. I invite you to stay true to the gospel written on our hearts by our Father, while thinking freely and questioning everything. Today, we are discouraged from defining our own beliefs and values. "It's the devil making you think that way." Maybe, but maybe not. Thinking freely can in fact bring us closer to God. Don't just go along with everything you hear. Read about it, pray, see what Father has to say to you. What makes my aunt different from my friends and spiritual leaders I've gone to concerning my mental health? For one, she's a Board Certified Psychiatric Mental Health Dr. of Nurse Practice and knows that mental illness is not something you can make up and she understands that trauma is a huge factor in a lot of my sexual confusion and growing acceptance of it. She's actually willing to work with me in that healing process. Instead of running away or dousing me with fuel to hate myself more, she is compassionate. When I talk with her, I'm talking to my best friend. I hear Jesus in everything she shares with me. What an honor it is to know the princess of our great God. Let her be an example to you, my dearests, treat others with love and grace. I am confident that another suicide attempt has been avoided. I will not lie, I think about it often, but the mercy she's granted me and the faith she's had in God throughout my process, restrains me from completing the act as I've intended all those times before. So Big Mommy, I thank you!

CHAPTER 5.
I Cried!

Never underestimate the impact you make in the lives of people around you.

At the beginning of this year, I truly heard in my spirit that this year is about the millennials, Gen Zs' who are going to change the trajectory of our world. Little did I know that we would be hit by COVID19, and the rise of Systemic Racism would impact our global communities. After reading my nephew's chapter 4 and what he wrote about me, I couldn't help but cry! Let me first thank him for seeing GOD in me. It is important that regardless of how we feel about any topic, LIVES MATTER. If we believe that lives matter, then we must really be willing to hear people out and make them count.

With all that is transpiring in the world these days, it is more important that we are very careful how we treat one another. This starts by not dismissing peoples' feelings and castrating them! This is what I hope that this book will do... to encourage us, bring back empathy which is even glaringly lacking in these days, understand that regardless of our own belief system ... we must not turn people into monsters. I truly love my nephew. I love all GOD's people.

Our differences are what make us unique but one is not better than the other. We were created in the likeness of ONE, the Creator. This is the base to start from.

I am very passionate about what I do as a board certified psychiatric mental health dr. of nurse practice. When patients come to my clinics, I do not see fault, I simply pray inward and ask God to show me how to help them. No one is perfect. I deal with Fibromyalgia, a very painful disease process; one that many still do not understand. When you tell someone how debilitating the pain can get, they think you are making it up. Even some primary care providers will tell you, it's an exaggeration in your mind. Some will tell you; your pain is not really real… it is in your head… all in your head. So, they prescribe antidepressant, anti-anxiety medications because they do not know what to say or do. Why am I sharing this, I KNOW! I know the pain of when you are trying to tell someone how you feel and they are telling you, what is going on is not real.

I am grateful that I have the support of a wonderful husband, children, sisters, brothers, nephews, nieces, brothers-in-law, mother, father who support me in this painful journey. I share my gifting with my nephew in this book, to reach out to those who are not that fortunate. I have patients who are under 17 years of age, their parents drop them at the door of the clinic and do not bother to come in to support their children who are finally seeking help after several years of mental torture. While I do not understand that, I do not judge it but simply there for the patient. In the same token, I have seen parents of my patients, finally come in after seeing vast improvement in their children… they come in to thank the provider, that is *moi*, for helping their children.

We are in no space to even judge one another yet we proceed without remorse.

Over twenty-five years ago, I tried to take my own life! No-one was there when I tried to plunge my car down the Verrazano bridge in New York. I hid my pain from my immediate family members because I felt like a failure. I had lost my home, my businesses, I was being dragged to three courts across Manhattan New York, Brooklyn New York, and New Jersey for divorce illegal proceedings yet the culprit was never caught or punished. It was the worst times of my life. Then, in the midst of this chaos, I was fighting hard to hold on to my two precious boys! It was finished for me, or so I thought! Could I ever trust again? When the one I loved from youth turned around and slapped me in the face with my love? How could I trust anyone else when the mother cunningly served me with divorce papers, then lied to the courts that she had served me divorce papers and had explained that she was serving me that. How could I trust again when his sisters, I had truly loved and devoted time, money towards their special days and did not have the decency to look beyond their brothers' money to do the right thing? I constantly ruminated over the questions; would they have accepted it, if the shoes were on the other foot... would their mother been okay if her daughter was thrown down the stairs by her husband? Would his mother be okay if her daughters' family money was swindled and used to open another business, then kicked out of her own business? How would she feel if her daughter was called every ugly name in the book and left disgraced in the community?

I spent years just ruminating over all of these while I watched as my ex lied his way through a lot. Up until that time, I had never thought of contemplating suicide. I was a social worker... I had dealt with mothers who were on drugs and left their children to fend for themselves. I had dealt with families who were struggling to make ends meet; those who were suffering from the AIDs virus and were and still are shamed in their communities. I did not meet the criterion of those who will choose attempted suicide as the way out. No-one would have ever thought I would be the one to try that route.

As a Nigerian Princess, my parents never allowed us to lack. So, my coming to America was not because we were suffering but more of gaining knowledge to take back home to Nigeria and Africa as a whole; thereby impacting my continent. But as it stands, GOD had a different plan for my life. I have stayed in this country, America for over 25 years now... had no plans to remain here but as fate would have it, it has enabled me to bridge the gap between both continents especially in the areas of health disparities and politics.

While my nephew tells me that he is experiencing compassion from me, I have no choice. This is the fabric of who I am. My parents (Abdul Rahman's grandparents) have taught us to put others first. They trained us to lend forgiveness even when it is incredibly difficult. They have trained us not to read meaning into things without taking our time to find out more about the persons involved. With my parents, they have trained us to understand that ALL MEN AND WOMEN are equal.

Growing up in Nigeria, we had helpers, those who some people would call "maids". But in our household, it was difficult to know who is a helper or my parents' children. At some point, there were over 23 people living in our home. All of our helpers went to school and when they graduated, they were set up with whatever they wanted to do. My parents had a rule of thumb, you finish high school first, then decide if you want to go to university or trade school. It was their choice. Some opted for college while some trade school.

It is my heart desire that Abdul Rahman's story and my commentaries will inspire, motivate, empower and thrust our readers into finding solutions to wherever they are; that these stories will engage those who are closed minded into rethinking their stance so that they can begin the journey of empathy and compassion towards others. It is equally my hope that this book will engage our global community into discussions that will yield favorable outcomes where treating patients who are suffering from mental illness is concerned.

The world will never be a healing place until we start to operate in Compassion and Empathy. This starts with leadership.

As a leader in my field as well as notable in the governmental and political sphere in Nigeria, it is imperative that we lead by great examples. This is where I believe I stand and my drive for helping my nephew to launch his own platform, starting with this book. I truly believe that all I went through in life, all of the successes and failures; all of the ups and downs, and where I am as a publisher myself … is for today; where I am now able to help launch my nephew and every other Abdul Rahman out there. If you are reading this, we need your help in ensuring that we reach other Abdul Rahman in any man or woman who may be struggling with mental illness and even sexual confusion.

There are times it takes YOU really going through things to understand the plight of others. On the other hand, if we practice compassion and empathy, it is not about what we go through but about placing others in ahead of us.

A wise man once told me this about myself:
*Princess, you were **manufactured** in Nigeria;*
*You were **assembled** in America;*
*Now, you are **dispatched** to the world.*
This adage has continued to be my vision torch. Whatever I do, where ever I go, I am constantly taking the temperature of who I am and what I do and ask the most pivotal question, have a veered off this message or am I still on track? My writings are my legs to the world, my documentaries are equally vehicles I use in pushing the message of compassion and empathy into the world.

Today, I pass the baton to my nephew and all the other Abdul Rahman's who are lurking in the dark. He is indeed a prolific writer that I am very proud of. My other nephews and nieces, my goodness, are equally prolific writers. I am so proud of them all, as I know they are very proud of Abdul Rahman now.

Often, I hear people discriminate against names like Muslim names like Abdul Razaaq, Abdul Rahman, and Zainab. They hear their names and automatically think they are terrorists. As a result, some in Nigeria, have even been burnt alive for what they did not do. Judgement belongs to GOD. We are in no space to even judge one another yet we proceed without remorse.

I look at the last four years in America, and it has been an incredibly painful experience, especially when we have leaders, more like clowns/masquerades who are relentlessly seeking to destroy their young and anyone who gets in their way. What is equally damming to me is watching those in leadership lambast one another and those who do not believe in their "nonsensical rantings." We have a leader disrespect other on a daily basis with his racists' comments, yet they run after him blindly, support him, help to clean up his words! American politics today has been riddled with consistent lies, derailment, confusion, and total chaos. It is quite sad times in America but the good news is that American citizens have the right to vote in and they equally have the right to vote out.

In the case of COVID19, we continue to see more deaths because people are not social distancing neither are they wearing their masks. I see on a daily basis, patients who are experiencing increased social phobia, heightened anxiety, seemingly unsurmountable depression. It is more of the getting locked in and out that is leading to the fatigue people are experiencing and not in the way it has been portrayed by leaders. We have leaders who put white house corona task force together to find solutions, have them release the solutions, then turn around to raise defiant people to disengage from the policies. They themselves, disengage from the solutions that were laid out by the task force.

Where systemic racism is concerned, well, that is yet another story. Our leader who is supposed to be leading the whole country, decides he will only lead the police and ignore the lives that had been lost aimlessly because of few bad apples in the police force, a force that truly needed to be cultured, re-trained, disciplined and help to do their jobs the right way.

I was a Social Worker in the heart of New York City prior to my life as a Psychiatric Mental Health Dr, of Nurse Practice. I love my police family, they helped me move in and out of some difficult places where my assigned families were. I also know that many of them are fatigued and not properly vetted before being employed. When caught in circumstances which needed to be investigated, they were protected heavily and some of them continue to fly under the radar till they retire because of the pension. True leaders will not take sides, rather, they will look into things carefully, tell the truth when necessary and tackle corruption, regardless. This is not what we are experiencing in today's America.

Many of my current patients come to me for post-traumatic stress syndrome (PTSD). I am known as Your Compassionate Trauma Care Maestro™. As we move through the COVI19 pandemic, I am seeing more people with COVID19 Fatigue Syndrome, which can also be called Acute Stress Syndrome. In addition, there is so much explosive anger and irritation which are components of these disease processes, anxiety, panic disorder, and depression. Those with narcissistic and socio-pathic tendencies are displaying their disorders for the world to see. What is more dangerous is allowing such tendencies to gain power over the country. Be on the watch out for my book on this.

So, I cry! I cry for our country America whose character has truly been on the global chopping block! The world is watching and seeing our position drop from being world leader and trail blazer to being behind in almost everything.

Africa especially Nigeria is not exempted from all of these corruptions. Nigeria has been in a very dark hole for the longest. We have a select group of people who toss the political ring amongst themselves, get to the position only to siphon the country's resources. The political race continues to become a very dangerous one, one in which the contestants would often cancel themselves out diabolically.

Abdul Rahman and I come from both worlds and studying both is really something. Today, its not much difference. However, we continue to be hopeful as mental health in both countries hinge upon our governments' reaction to it. Mental health is another pandemic which is ravishing through the countries.

CHAPTER 6.
Life on the Edge

The shadows and faces were alive and breathing like you and me. They never talked to me until my early 20s. It started out as benign, incoherent mumbling, and then I would hear my name being whispered.

WARNING: *This chapter is real, raw, and can be regarded as graphic to some. It is simply a recollection and is the personal experience of Abdul Rahman, a person diagnosed with Schizoaffective disorder. It is not meant to offer ways of attempting suicide but simply to offer recommendations to parents and family members who are dealing with a loved one who may be suffering from* **Schizoaffective disorder and Bulimia.**

In October of 2019, I genuinely thought my life was over. Sounds a bit too dramatic for a young man to say. After all, I'm not elderly and I "still have a future." I laughed and still do scoff at the idea of living long and getting married. I didn't want and often still don't want to. I was diagnosed with Schizoaffective Disorder; a combination of Schizophrenia and a major mood disorder such as Depression or Bipolar. *Great! Even worse,* I thought. But it did bring me some solace to finally have an answer to all the horrific things I've seen since I was a teenager. What horrid things have I seen? It ranged from shadows to grotesquely detailed faces on the walls and in the blinds on the window. They were faces of people I didn't know. I had lost touch with reality but hadn't known it. The shadows and faces were alive and breathing like you and me. They never talked to me until my early 20s. It started out as benign, incoherent mumbling, and then I would hear my name being whispered. It quickly progressed into deep voiced creatures commanding me to kill myself or pick up random objects while I was walking. They were unlike any other voice I've heard before. They were not human. The hallucinations have only gotten worse as I age. I saw my friend who had passed away only a few weeks prior, in the apartment of my other friend. I was grieving her death all the while dealing with hallucinations. I wish mental illness wasn't so insidious like that. Are ghosts real or was I hallucinating even as a child? I remember seeing my "aunt" Shelly in my room in my mom's apartment in New York when I was a kid. She was covered in rainbow light and was beautifully transparent. She died of breast cancer. Upon finding that out, I saw her that night. My friend, Katrina, died of colon cancer and she had deteriorated to the point where I couldn't recognize her. It hurt me deeply that she suffered in such an inhumane way. I was mad at God for the longest time. I thought He was sadistic and wanted to inflict the pain on my friend. What made me angrier were my classmates' response to it. "God is good." It made me sick… While I was mad at God over my friend's painful death, I began seeing severed heads and hands in my room, felt breathing on my neck, and bugs crawling on my skin. With everything going on at the time, I couldn't cope effectively so I began to cut myself again.

Cutting was my form of tension release. Seeing the blood trickle down my arm was like a warm hug. Whenever I'd drink, I'd have more boldness in cutting myself. Those scars are still visible on my upper arm today, from those nights of drinking.

They say suicide is a selfish act.

The cutting only intensified my suicidal ideation. I felt chained. I was trapped in the cycle of self- hatred and punishment. I wanted a way out. Who could've released me? So, I tried it all; from overdose to hanging. God wasn't done and is not done with my life yet. I often begged Him to take my life before I did, but God always came through and prevented my premature death. I can't say I'm grateful He didn't answer my prayer. I remember one of my most traumatic suicide attempts very vividly. It was September 6th, 2015 and I was downstairs in the basement of our house. I snuck away after deciding that it was the day to end things. My brother was in another room and my mom had been out of the house for a while. *The perfect chance*, I thought. I frantically grabbed two bottles of pain killers and took an amount that I knew would kill me and I told God, "I'm sorry...Please forgive me." What followed was the most serene sleep I've ever had. I'd venture to say I was actually comatose. I didn't have dreams. I was just in a thick black that seemed to last forever. I've never felt so calm in my life. As far as I was concerned, I was ready to go and felt in my heart that God would be willing to carry me home. A lot of people say that those who complete suicide, go to hell. Not only is this very insensitive to the family of a person who's completed suicide, it is also very unforgiving and ignorant. Does the saving grace of God only apply when you do the right thing all the time? I thought about my mom and my siblings up until I fell asleep. I had some regrets, but I was in far too much pain to continue on earth. I was completely out of my mind and was already in hell, living in this world. They say suicide is a selfish act. I'm inclined to disagree. People who complete suicide are not selfish but were severely mentally ill and they needed help. Our God should be understanding. I will further say that some who complete suicide or attempt to end their lives, actually felt like they were doing their loved ones a favor. They think of their loved ones more than they think of themselves or their pain. Tell me, how is that selfish? I recall many times I felt like a burden to my family because of how unwell I was. In fact, I remember my mom telling me, "You bring me grief," after I asked what about myself made her happy. This stuck with me and is one of the many reasons I wish to die, even now. I hate adding anymore pain to our world and since I'm not doing any good by being alive, I often feel that it's time to go. Imagine the anger I felt when I woke up. I remember so clearly saying out loud, "Ugh…Are you serious?!" As you learned earlier, I like to pretend that everything's fine. So, I went upstairs and my mom had come home, and I went to cut my hair and that was the end of that. I later found out I had severely damaged my liver and my kidneys. That didn't stop me from trying to die all the more though. Visions of a painful or swift end filled me with rapture. I often rehearsed my various suicide plans without anyone knowing. I had urges to lie in the road or jump in front of a car so I could be killed, and I actually did jump in front of a moving car but the driver stopped in the nick of time. I had a death wish and didn't want to be stopped. I remember wrapping my belt around my neck and positioning the belt in such a way so I could get it in the door and hang myself that way. God kept His covenant with my mom and has not allowed me to die despite the lethality of the methods I've tried. I told myself many times, that if my mother died, maybe I'd have more strength to end my life or my spirit would feel free enough to leave my body for good. At this moment, I'm living for my mother. However painful it is to stay on this earth, I will stay for her. I can't make any promises, after she's gone. I don't value myself that much and I don't believe anyone who says they value me now. I don't want to. Medication helps me not think about suicide as often as I did before. I'm grateful for that because when I'm suicidal, it's very frightening and overwhelming. I usually act swiftly on the plans that come into my head.

If it wasn't suicide that would end me, it was going to be Bulimia. I often wanted it to kill me. I knew the dangers. So, people telling me all the things that could happen to me didn't scare me and I was actually excited when my body would show signs of failing. My hair grew thin and fell out and my heart wasn't in good shape and I still deal with that today. I get chest pains whenever I walk, and breathing is so difficult. I never understood the people in my life who would say I should stop though. For one, I feel like I haven't suffered enough, and I couldn't stop unless I was constantly supervised. Also, why would I want my friend to leave me? Some of you may know exactly what I mean by "friend." My friend helped me escape my reality. My friend made me forget about the uncomfortable feelings I had about my sexuality because of our heteronormative society. My friend made me numb to the constant flashbacks of the sexual assault I experienced. Maybe if it hadn't happened, I would've never met her. Maybe your friend is alcohol, or it's pornography (I dealt with that for 14 years and I'll get into that later). People recover but maybe I won't and I'm okay with that. Don't know if I even want to recover from this eating disorder. Who would I be without it? I still deal with Depression after all. This eating disorder helps me cope. I can't say it is all that fun binging on thousands of calories of McDonald's burgers and Pizza, and local gas station food, in one sitting and purging violently though. I take a risk every time I purge. I could've died at any time, but it made me feel alive, for once. It gives me something to do. It gives me purpose and I feel accomplished if I have multiple episodes in one day even though it is very physically and emotionally taxing on me. *I'm good for nothing anyway. I might as well binge and purge,* I think to myself. I go into every binge/purge session knowing it will be my last, but it never is. I survive and I do it again and again. Instinct isn't wrong. God just preserved me all this while. At first, I had no goal when I first started struggling with Bulimia. As time when on though, I wanted to get back to my lowest weight and keep going lower so I could look unattractive. I didn't want to be abused again. If I was emaciated, I wouldn't be touched. That was my logic. It bothered me when church folk and even my own family told me I looked good. I wasn't trying to look good. At the heart of it, it isn't about weight at all. I binged and purged so I didn't feel the weight of the traumatic things I've experienced and carried out on others.

It always came back to the sexual assault. That's what fueled the decline I was in and am in. I had one period of remission (by no choice of my own) and I relapsed. I remember the night I relapsed so well. It was Halloween 2018 and I had just finished talking to my friends about trauma and we shared our experiences with each other. Something one of them said had triggered me and I was sent back to when I was 10 years old. I never felt so much disdain for myself in that moment. Looking in the mirror, something in my soul said, "You deserve it, b***h..." After which I stuck my fingers down my throat and purged. It didn't feel like me. Maybe it was, but the anger I felt was inhuman. To think I'd have mercy on that 10-year-old boy who was violated without any regard for his humanity, but I was infuriated at him. It was his fault. He shouldn't have said yes. This is the constant narrative playing in my head throughout this relapse and each session

I have becomes increasingly violent. Binging and purging is the medium I use to feel less and punish myself. No amount of cutting, binging and purging, or starving has ever satisfied my longing for retribution. I hold a grudge against myself for not only saying yes to the one who assaulted me, but for hurting others and desiring to hurt others in like manner. I cannot and will never forgive myself.

I feel like Beast from *Beauty and the Beast*. You might say, "He ended up changing though." Not me... I feel like I'm stuck this way. The thoughts I have are unnatural. They range from stabbing my neighbor to death and putting his blood all over me, to raping a woman just walking on the street. I haven't carried out any of my fantasies as of right now, but I fear myself. I often feel like I don't belong in our world for that very reason. I'm different. My abuser planted his evil seed in me, quite literally and I feel like I am obligated to carry on that curse of harming others without remorse. I sometimes feel I am bound to, as it was done to me. But I know better.

I don't cope very well as you have discovered already. So, what I'm about to say should come as no surprise to you. I was addicted to popping pills. The pills I'd take were over the counter pain killers, and when I could get a hold of them, prescription pain killers like Vicodin and Hydrocodone. You might wonder how I had access to these pills. I stole them. No, I didn't shoplift. I simply took what was already in our house, without anyone looking. It was exciting to be sneaky and take 4 of my stepdad's prescription pills that he used after leg surgery. I was anxious that he wouldn't get anymore, and my supply would run short. I always prayed he got more of his prescription from the pharmacy and sure enough, he did. Each time I'd overdose on OTC pain killers, my heart would beat fast and the chest pain I experienced was unreal. I would wake up and the schizoaffective disorder would flare up in the sense that my hallucinations became even more intense.

Besides pill popping, I was addicted to pornography. I was first exposed to it when I was 12 years old and my family and I were in a hotel in the Netherlands. I was flipping through channels innocently and I heard moaning and saw two women touching each other. I didn't understand what I was seeing but my mom came in the room and quickly took hold of the remote and changed the channel. I'm grateful for that moment. No child should see that kind of thing. I was already infected. When we went back to the United States, a year had passed, and I was 13. While I was at school that year, one of my friends started moaning and my body became excited and he showed me a website he was on, in the middle of class. I went home that day and I searched on, *On Demand,* (part of a comcast service we had at the time) and I came out of my body. I started scrolling through the adult section out of curiosity. I didn't know it, but I was pressing, the "Buy" option before watching the pornographic films. What I'd seen, horrified me, a young boy. I was so scared, and I looked to see if anyone was in the house as the volume was loud. When I say I was scared, I mean I was really terrified. I wasn't terrified of being caught; I was more afraid of what I was seeing. It was too much for my eyes. My good spirit was marred. One day my mom came home, and it was judgment day. I had given my mom a bill of $1,000 and some, because I watched pornography. What followed was beating. The following day or so, my mom asked me while we were both in the car, "Who did you think was gonna pay for all this? Answer me…" I replied, "I don't know…Daddy?" Then she did something I didn't expect.

She pulled over and demanded that I get out of the car and walk home. I'll never forget that day. Till this day, I fear anytime my mom presses on the brake in a car because I feel like she'll leave me on the side of the road again. I was abandoned. I cried as she sped off. I didn't want to forgive her for the longest time. As I'm writing this, the feelings are still fresh. I was prey to anyone who wanted to hurt me. They had the perfect opportunity. I was ripe for slaying and sexual torture. She knew that... I remember a man staring at me while I was crying. I began my trek home. I didn't know where home was from there. I was lost. The relief I felt when I saw my mom's car was fleeting. I was livid. I wanted to ask her, "How could you leave me?" The ride home was a quiet one. I didn't want to talk to her. Not after that stunt she pulled. The next 13 years was filled with shame, suicidal thoughts, and fatigue as I couldn't stop watching pornography no matter what I tried. It took a long while for me to even begin healing from that. I noticed a pattern. When I would seek out pornographic videos online, the videos were typically featuring women in the positions I was in when I was sexually assaulted at 10 years old and molested at 14. Each time I watched pornography; I was retraumatized. When I was in my 20s, after watching pornography, I would engage in eating disorder behaviors to forget about and numb the pain I felt watching people having grotesque sex. I could see myself in every woman.

CHAPTER 7.
I Will Not Shut My Eyes…

You took my breath and said, "His death can't wait…" You smother my people with your hard knees. I swallowed cement after you slaughtered every one of my lambs. What gave you such power? You raped us for it; you vipers and depraved bastards. You stole our tongues; you stole our right to learn and you stole our minds. I cannot sleep. I will not shut my eyes. Not before my people matter, like you all say they do. "All lives matter." We don't matter right now; so that statement is not only a lie but an insult to the thousands of my ancestors who were lashed without mercy, whose mouths were padlocked all for the vile pleasure of a white man and his soul hungry demon brigade. Here onward, you will starve. Every single one of you without a heart for my people, black people. Restore our children with education that you freely offered my White brothers and sisters! Use the taxes we pay, to lift up my children. Pay our teachers in the inner city. Equip us with books containing real history. Give back what you plundered from our palace, that is our heart. What are you afraid of?! Give us our dreams that you threw away in effort to curb rebellion. I can't unsee the evil you've done to me, a thousand times over. I am not imagining the plight of my people and you know it. I will not shut my eyes to what you've done until you're held accountable. Zion is crying. Her blood was spilled and I say from today, you will answer for it.

"I died when they died"

I AM Emmett Till, Breonna Taylor, Tony McDade, Trayvon Martin, Eric Garner, Michael Brown, George Floyd, Ahmaud Arbery, and too many to name without crying. I will not retract my statement. I died when they died, and I die every single day that you kill my brother and my sister for no just reason. What you're telling me is, I don't matter to anyone. You're telling me and every dying black man and woman, that our value is determined by a white man or woman who wants to keep crushing our heads and remain on top. Why shouldn't I take my life if all I am is a number to an officer and to a judge? For a long time, I couldn't watch the news. It's yet more trauma I and my brothers and sisters have to recover from. Watching the death of our daddy and our friend, George Floyd, over and over again, did not do us any good. Videos of his murder spread like wildfire and there was nowhere I could escape to, to find my breath. I still can't breathe. I threw up in my mouth when I saw the George Floyd challenge circulating. I was livid. It was not and is not funny, what happened to him. It's not only traumatic when we see our loved ones die, it's also traumatic when we witness no justice.

Breonna Taylor's case should be fresh in all our minds. Need I remind you? She was a 26-year-old ER technician who was in her own home along with her boyfriend when officers executed a search warrant on the WRONG home. Let that sink in. I'll wait... What's disturbing about this case is that they entered the home without knocking which prompted Breonna's boyfriend to start shooting at what he believed were intruders. The officers fired their weapons in response and killed Breonna Taylor. She was innocent. Innocent...One of the officers who shot at Breonna was charged for bullets that were found in a nearby apartment but not Breonna's. Every year, we are reminded of how much we don't matter. It really affects my mental health. I'm afraid to go outside. When I see American flags, my heart races. I pledged to this same flag I am now afraid of. What it means to be American has changed and not for the better. To be American now is to be White, look down on immigrants, and follow President Trump and all his ideals. Anytime I go on a walk, I fear the police being called. Heaven forbid I come across them. I'm a target. I'm black, have a long beard, and ever-growing hair.

To our standing president and whomever should follow him….

To our standing president and whomever should follow him, you are unrighteous if you do not seek justice for the poor and use the scepter our Father has given you to declare sin as sin and decree punishment on those who treat the vulnerable and minorities as less than human. It hurts me that President Trump cannot stand to condemn the vile acts of white supremacists in America. The delivering of nooses to our doors must stop. The threats on social media directed towards African American protesters, must also stop. I call for the abolishment of the KKK. Any organization which stands to keep the white race superior by any means necessary, must be dealt with according to the law and any new law that shall be passed. Give us back our fathers… Why should they stay in jail for years over a simple drug offense? You've caged my people far too long and I say in the words of our great God, "Let my people go…" Mr. President, let my people go, NOW. Pardon the sins of a multitude who fear God. You also must be forgiven. You've been drunk with our blood and sustain your life by drawing from the well of our tears. Enough is enough.

"To White Supremacists..."

To White Supremacists, what bothers you about us? Is it our stubborn resilience? You snuffed out our young, but we will continue to multiply. We will grow mightier as our people fall to your sword. We know who's on our side? You're fighting a losing battle. We will not stay in the gutter that you've cursed. We will rise above the reproach.

To Black People: Cloak of Shame and Reproach

Today, I'm taking the cloak of shame, reproach, and grief off of my people, black people. Our enemies will not rejoice over us. The LORD YHWH will answer every one of them for laughing at our misfortune. Please, do not settle for less. You are more than disability checks, welfare, 9-5's with low pay, and inpatient psychiatric hospital stays. You deserve far more than what you lived with. This is what keeps us bound.

It's hard getting a job these days as people in high power look at our foreign, peculiar names and say, "They aren't worth anything. They won't do well in our company." I actually used a white name to see if I'd get a call back from the same job I applied to and was rejected at. They called back. I encourage you to be innovative. Don't settle for working for other people. You've faced enough violence at the hands of those you've worked for, many years ago. It's time they buy from a hardworking people. We toil and shed tears for the prize they always find a way of taking from us. Many of you are waiting for promotion. Again, I say, be innovative. Sell jewelry, cook, sell your produce that is from your farm. You have great potential and I know you're capable of living your best life like the white man is. How we get to where we are will be judged soon. Press on towards the prize, my friends. Do not give up. We've been scorned for years and like my Jewish friends, have become accustom to it. It's so easy to let the burden of unwantedness, weigh us down. My spirit has also been crushed under the weight of that. We are naked babes to our oppressors. Our God is bigger than them.

"We need counselors on our streets..."

With the death of yet another black man in America, it's clear that police do NOT know what they're doing. Walter Wallace was clearly severely distraught and needed compassion and careful handling. As a crisis counselor, it's our protocol to show empathy and to always de-escalate instead of aggravating the client with harsh commands or not showing a great deal of patience. Pointing a gun at someone with a knife will only make them more agitated and defensive. We don't need police going to mental health calls or calls involving minority youths in distress. There should be a special group of people chosen by the state or a local private hospital to handle mental health crises on the streets. Here's my message to police: Until you learn to stand down and use your voice to calm people down, you're fired.

SARS, Protests, and Police Brutality

I am not blind to what my people do to themselves. It saddens me that lawlessness and greed is the god of the Nigerian police force. SARS was an extension of the Nigerian police force. They specialized in curbing armed robbery which is very common in Nigeria. Along the way, SARS became terroristic. In my humble opinion, SARS is in the ranks with Boko Haram and Al Qaeda. It's hard to look through my twitter feed. Graphic videos and images flood my screen further traumatizing me. I recall a video my mom showed me of dead bodies with broken bones and severed hands. SARS was responsible for it. Sadly, we grow desensitized to violence. Videos like the one my mom showed me, keeps spreading. SARS is responsible for sodomizing and raping my youth and adults in Nigeria. They are criminals and need to be stopped. As my dear brother, Abdul Razaaq, would say, "There are enough bad apples to question the orchard." In response to all the happenings, youth from around the world banded together to put an end to SARS. While SARS is separate from the police force now, they are still active and police brutality is still an issue in Nigeria. I remember seeing a barbaric murder of a bus driver on the streets of Nigeria at the hands of an officer. They were arguing about money. In Nigeria, unlike the United States, there are no laws against bribery and officers will actually demand you to give them money. Especially when they find out you're a foreigner or from the West. The officer broke the glass of the driver window and dragged the bus driver out and beat him on the head with a black baton. He was lifeless and the officer continued to beat him. It was a traumatic thing to witness but it was just another day in Nigeria.

At one of the protests, the Nigerian Army and Nigerian Police open fire on unarmed youths. The sound of multiple gunshots is still ringing in my ears. The people were of no threat to anyone and simply speaking their truth. They are tired. They are martyrs for the cause of annulling corruption in high places. They did not die in vain.

"It's a heart issue...."

It's not just a white vs black or a black vs. black issue. It's a heart issue. I will never deny that racism exists, because it does. We must get the full picture. At the core of it is the truth that we are depraved and are capable of the evilest things. Ask me how I know... People oft comfort themselves by saying, "I'm not like them. They're really bad people." Or still some of you are saying, "I'd never do anything like that!" None of us are better than Hitler. We're all in need of much mercy from God. Hear me out...I remember being let go at my former job. After I was let go, I remembered I had a pocketknife in my pants pocket, and I wanted to stab the person who gave me a rude look. I thought better of it only because I fear the law. I was so close to doing it. Maybe some of you have had similar situations occur in your life. Your wife nags you constantly about whatever and in every argument, you wish you could hit her and you inch towards her. Maybe you're not violent. But maybe you lock your car door anytime a black man walks by in the parking lot. Perhaps you've crossed the street when you see a man with tattoos walking behind you. Why do you look the other way when a man or woman who has no home, stands at the corner of a gas station? That too is an evil thing to do. I will not lie about this; I will actually say I am evil by my example. Give yourself enough time and demand honesty from yourself and you will find that you are evil too. So, what we do about it? I reckon we go back to the cleanser of hearts, JESUS.

CHAPTER 8.
The Poison of Secrecy

Mental illness thrives in secrecy. It feeds off our fear of being vulnerable. As you know by now, I like to keep things under wraps until things reach a crisis point. We shouldn't have to reach crisis point before we get help. Problem is though, some actually do reach out before a crisis and they're not taken seriously. It sickens me how Depression, Anxiety and eating disorders in young people are often perceived as teenage angst or seen as childish. You wonder why a 10-year-old hangs themselves in a closet? Consider your response to their many cries about their pain. Perhaps you've said to your 11-year-old daughter, "What do you have to be depressed about? You're selfish. You should be grateful." Or to your 13-year-old son who's being bullied, "Stop crying. Just ignore them." Comments like these only make us retreat and not want to talk to anyone. If you've reached out to people and they've said similar things to you, I'm so sorry.

Over the years, I've learned the importance of reaching out to the right people. But who are the right people? Humans are bound to fail us! After hearing my experiences with religious people, you might be saying, "Don't go to the church!" There are good people in church just as much as there are also parasites and leeches among the congregants. So, who is trustworthy? I encourage you to not allow one heart wrenching experience to discourage you from seeking the help that you need and deserve. I've been told I was attention seeking by my mother and my sister. This is why I'm very careful about not going to them to discuss my mental health in depth, no matter how much I love them. I can't allow them into my secret place. I was also criticized for sharing I had nightmares. An aunt of mine once said to me something along the lines of, "How old are you that you're having nightmares?" I learned to speak Christianese when talking with most of my family and church friends. That's what they want to hear, and I can't blame them. No one is comfortable with pain. Let people prove themselves to you before you let them in on your struggles. If you're not careful, some would use that trouble you're experiencing, against you. I used to be an open book. There was nothing I wouldn't share if you asked, "How are you?" But with each response I gave, I learned that no one really wants to hear the truth of your answer.

Where do you start with speaking about your pain? I found that the internet has been a great resource for me in sharing my melancholy and thought processes. I tried online therapy for a while and it was helpful even though it became too much for my bank account. I'm so glad to have a therapist who understands me. Her name is Alexis. She's helped me so much. I've tried many therapists and have gone to advance practice nurses, and none of them were really helpful. In fact, there are a few in particular who really hurt me. On my first appointment at her office, one Nigerian APN wanted to send me inpatient because of the frequency of my purging. She coined the idea to me as a threat. As if that wasn't enough, she guilted me for my suicide attempts and insinuated that I was selfish for acting on my suicidal impulses. "Think of how your mother would feel. That's very selfish of you." I knew that I couldn't keep seeing her. Then I saw a social worker who was in her 60s. I became a counselor to her. On top of that, she made it a point to act shocked that I was mentally ill. "You look so put together; I would've never known you went through something so crazy." It may take a while to find the right person you can vibe with, enough to start healing. Once you do though, you'll be glad you opened up.

I can't end this chapter without saying who has been there for me the most when I needed someone. I encourage you to try Him out. Jesus is my life source and without Him, I am nothing. He is so forgiving and trustworthy. You don't have to try and be perfect before you come to Him. Just be who you are and brutally honest. He admires a truth seeker and those who chase after Him diligently. I promise, God will find you if you keep reaching out to Him. He's always available to help and to love on you.

CHAPTER 9.
COVID19 and the Other Pandemics

It's hard to combat the lies you're told while you're in isolation.

No one saw it coming. Its sinister presence made us shudder for our elderly or our aging parents and brought us into a deeper abyss. Jobs were put on hold and people were forced to stay home. Where was money going to come from? People lost every sense of security when this virus came on the scene. Restrictions prevented people from going out and de-stressing at dance clubs or watching movies at the theater. Granted, the plague was and is still out there but staying home has done us more harm than good. This is what President Trump and I agree on. What I don't agree with is his constant downplaying of the crisis at hand, which I will address later. A lot of us, including myself, already struggled with isolation before everything went to crap around the world. I'd spend a lot of time in my room. It was my "safe space," but it was hurting me. My room was often darkened by pillows I would place by the windows. I didn't want light. I hated light. I cursed the morning every time I saw the sun; even if it was raining. I just hated being awake. It's hard to combat the lies you're told while you're in isolation. Many of us are in Depression imposed quarantine. We feel like infectious diseases to our families and our friends because of our state of mind. We think, "No one wants me here," or "I'm too broken for this world. It can go on without me." Even with actual quarantine ending in a majority of states in the US, some of us are still in that headspace. When I was in quarantine, my eating disorder and

Depression spiraled and very quickly. I woke up every single day, demanding that I died. I didn't want to be here. Imagine being told, "You're disgusting, you're worthless, no one loves you," while trapped in your house with the people that supposedly love you. Can you picture the unrelenting paranoia I felt? I couldn't trust my sister or my mom even though I love them dearly. My eating disorder had free reign in my life during quarantine. Food was easily accessible at home and from fast food joints. I just had to say, "I'm going to the park," and I was alone with Bulimia. Bulimia helped me cope during that time of uncertainty and maybe Anorexia, drinking, pill popping, is helping you now. It was hard to find a different coping mechanism. Nothing was as good as stuffing my face full of food and throwing up. Nothing else felt as right. It felt natural. Bulimia gave me the chance to breathe. After each purge, I had a sense of finality. I felt like something was ending. Even if it wasn't COVID19, I felt calm. As quickly as I felt calm, my fear returned. I really wanted COVID to be over. I couldn't go to work because I lost my job and I couldn't go to school because I was focusing on bettering my mental health. I felt awful for not being accomplished in some way. I wanted to do something and be something for once and COVID was in the way of that.

"I was in prison..."

I recall pressing my hand on the window, especially on the days it would rain, and I'd beg God for the sun just so I could go on a walk. The silence in my head was enough and I couldn't bear another day inside a quiet house. I was in prison and I needed my shackles to be destroyed. My mother often worked nights when COVID first started. The urges I had to cut myself were so high, but I did not act on them for fear that my mom would check my arms at random. I was alone but not alone. My sister also began to disintegrate into a familiar madness. If I could've cried, I would have but every numbing agent I used prevented and continues to shield me from tears I would not be able to stop. We all meet insanity at various points of our lives, and some are crushed under the pressure of its voice. "Take off your clothes.' 'Call the police and charge at them with a knife so they could kill you.'" That's what I heard the voice say many times over and occasionally I actively listen. Maybe, the voice you hear says "Stay in bed all day,' or 'Just one more pill than you usually take.'" COVID19 is hellish and even those who have no symptoms are in its grip. COVID's hands has gripped the nations and its iron scepter cries out for the death of every man, woman, and child. Whether that death is as a result of the virus itself or suicide. It will happen. What has protected you all this while? Our God says we should multiply and COVID19 is seeking to depopulate the world. This is not a conspiracy. One third or more of the population of our precious world will perish under COVID19's edict. This is serious. Now is not the time for division. We must come together and stop this evil. Please, stop picking sides. "I'm Democrat.' 'I'm Republican.'" We are THE PEOPLE, first and foremost. Never forget that. A house divided against itself can never and will never stand.

"COVID19 is REAL...."

I will not allow shame to push me into a darker silence. I've been quiet for far too long.

President Trump's denial of the health crisis in our country is appalling and disturbing. America, COVID19 is REAL... In case you didn't already know, our death toll is climbing by the minute. People are dying. Our president very well could've been in that number. Does our president not know the power in his voice? He mocks the virus and still has the audacity to say that it doesn't kill young people. Someone at church whom I talked to one day actually said the same thing. Mr. President, please, mind your language. People listen to what you say and take it for gospel. Do not lead your sheep astray. I see many on Facebook claiming that, "It's not dying from the virus that's the problem, it's dying without Christ." I will not deny the seriousness of the issue that is living a life that is not Christ centric and dying without the Spirit's seal.

However, this does not change the fact that people are dying from this illness at alarming rates. The ignorance and foolish faith of religious people really bothers me. A lot of these same people refuse to wear masks or complain about it and claim what's going on isn't that serious. Stop claiming your right to religious freedom when talking to someone about mask wearing. If you were truly a Christian, you'd obey the law of the land. How does wearing a mask impede on your freedom? Nowhere in scripture does it say, "Thou shalt not wear a mask." I get that you want to be with your friends and party or whatever. Keep this in mind though, your life is not worth one party that you'll likely forget about in a week. You should also be mindful and wear a mask because of the people in your life who are especially susceptible to the virus. You really don't want to bring the virus to your home. You care less about something that doesn't personally affect you. It's a fact. Do you hear that? That's the sound of true infirmity. Minimization and denial are fatal sicknesses. So many are carriers of it.

SUICIDE....

Own Your Stories.

You won't hear many talking about this, as it's kind of a hush hush matter. I will not be quiet. Doctors, nurses, and mental health technicians are completing suicide. Our soldiers were in the trenches of a serious battle. Not just the COVID19 pandemic, they were also tormented by bitter melancholy and violent terror. We need not put our doctors or medical professionals on pedestals that make us presume they have everything under control. We view our healthcare workers as superheroes. Please keep in mind, even superheroes bleed. They are not immune to losing themselves in unspeakable sorrow or fear. Healthcare workers also need a cure and tender care. This isn't something a vaccine can fix. So, while we narrow in on a vaccine for COVID, we should also be wise by making sure that our doctors, our nurses, and whomever else are actually okay. I propose bi-monthly psych evaluations for those in the health care field. They need our love just as much as we need their hands and their minds which God uses to heal us. Suicide is the 2nd leading cause of death in people aged 10-34. According to data from WHO (World Health Organization), every 20 seconds, someone completes suicide. In the years prior, WHO recorded that every 40 seconds, someone completes suicide. The rate of death has increased. We have a serious problem. I survived a plethora of suicide attempts. There are not enough words to describe the anger, and guilt I feel about this. Too many have died. What makes me so darn special? What do we do about this crisis on our hands? I propose that we start killing shame.

The Power of Shame

Shame…It's what keeps our families in the dark. It's ultimately what kills us. Maybe you too have met your fair share of religious people, or your family just isn't understanding or compassionate. I understand why you'd fall into addiction, dear brother or sister. Shame perpetuates the narrative in our minds that we are bad people for something we can't control. I have so much shame around my attractions. *People would kill me upon my confession,* I thought to myself; *not even a priest could forgive me.* I told one person and they're now out of my life. Leaving that conversation, I felt like I was the vilest creature on earth. I wasn't even human in my mind. I was a beast. The ways in which some of us respond to the pain of our friends can contribute to shame.

Bulimia is a graphic, disgusting, violent, eating disorder.

Feeling out of control with the eating disorder and observing the disgust of some family and friends added to my overall sense of shame. It's one of the reasons I don't talk about it to anyone. It would be easier to talk if I dealt with Anorexia. The media talks about it a lot and it's more understood. I hate to use this word but it's much more graceful than Bulimia. Bulimia is a graphic, disgusting, violent, eating disorder. Let's be honest…

Some of you are familiar with the phrase, "You brought shame to the family." We joke about it when it comes to Asian Americans and school, or when they come out as gay. It's not only an Asian issue. I feel this pressure to keep my own family together so those abroad don't laugh at my mom. Everything I've written in this book thus far, is my truth and will bring controversy. This will shake my family and the world will ask questions. But I will not allow shame to push me into a darker silence. I've been quiet for far too long.

Shame and suicide are best friends. When I attempted suicide, I felt shame for not being the model son and brother. I felt shame for my sexual preferences. I felt shame for everything I've ever done to anyone. Shame makes us hide from the light. It makes us isolate. Shame offers no hope of redemption. "We are who we are, and we can't change." That's what shame says. If I couldn't change who I was and who I was is unacceptable in our society, I had to kill myself. I had no other options. I was petrified of opening up even to people I trusted. I feared that if I did, they would see all of me. They would see the part of me I've been trying to bury for decades. I couldn't look people in the eyes when I would lay my heart down. Shame is responsible for that. What you try to bury, will rise to the surface or worst-case scenario, bury you. We have to let go of our shame to fully heal. That doesn't mean not having regret, but we must realize that what we've been through and what we've done is a part of our story. Today, I encourage all of you to own your stories. They are unique and beautiful however thorny it has gotten at times.

CONCLUSION

Manufactured in Nigeria, West Africa.
Assembled in United States of America.
Dispatched to the World.
One Event Can Change Your Life Forever.

This has truly been an incredible journey for me; helping my nephew birth his vision mission and goal. Likewise, bringing awareness and putting a face to mental illness especially in silent cultures like African, Latinos, African Americans, and other developing countries. With the uproar in America these days, it is important that we do not allow the noises to drown what's important. Mental Illness kills! We cannot ignore this fact and so, it is vital that we act

My nephew mentioned previously that quarantining has increased the mental illness amongst Americans. While this is absolutely true, I see it slightly from a different point of view. Our mental stability is being challenged because our leadership keeps ignoring it, keeps perpetrating the lies about it literally not being a big thing; exposing others to the virus recklessly, and delaying peoples healing. If people were made to understand the importance of following the mandate at the onset, we probably would have been a long way now. When budget is being cut, it is amazing to see that mental health and social work are usually the first to be considered for cut. With where America or even the global communities are going, it is important that we must bring mental illness to the front. As a practicing Psychiatric Mental Health Dr. of Nurse Practice, I see a lot of immigrants in Arizona suffering from mental illness. The truth is that many are severely mentally ill because they were never treated growing up due to cultural bias and the stigma associated with mental illness. I remember a 58 years old Hispanic man who walked into my clinic. At 58, he had lived most of his life in prison. He told me that the only years he had lived outside of confinement has beeb10 years combined. Every time he was released, he got into trouble by fighting and he is them send back to the prison. He had been given an ultimatum by the wife to go seek mental health and stay out of trouble. This visit was the most crucial of his life, he was ashamed, felt guilty and explained how he dare not go back to his community with everyone knowing about his mental illness. It was one thing to be accused of being bipolar but it was another for reality to be in display. He was quite guarded and paranoid. After long discussion with him, he felt confident about pursuing his treatment with me. At the end of the day, we were once again faced with another challenge… it was the issue of not using medication, as that was not believed mostly in his cultural background. In fact, he told me that his family cannot know about all of these but his immediate family. His wife was alright with using medication. The types of taboos are not investigated well in America. Arizona is ripe for such research as we have the American Indians, The Latinos, African and the Black Americans. It is my hope that my clinics will begin to explore such differences as we use rehabilitative writing to bring healing.

This book, we hope has certainly brought healing to you, the individual, transformation to our communities at large. Rahman and I hope it has brought to light what it looks, like to be dealing with mental illness, we implore compassion and empathy. Looks are deceiving. We must learn to be patient with one another, seek to understand each other, believe that we are uniquely created and that we each have our destinies to fulfill. Despite our individual calling, we are still all closed knitted. Many of our destinies are tied to one another and when one does not move, the other parts do not move either. We are important to one another and so we must exercise empathy and much patients.

For a country to succeed, it must never entertain narcissism and sociopathic leadership. Condoning bad behavior is destructive to the society at large. Regardless of our creed, religion, social status, gender, we must appreciate one another and lift each other up rather than tear reach others. My nephew, Rahman, tells me how scared he is when he leaves the house because of all the systemic racism- young men being massacred on the streets. When a black or Latino mother sends the son out, she warns him about not using the hoody. He reminds him to raise his hands whenever a cop tries to stop him. A Caucasian mother is not thinking of these things. Change starts with us… the individual. It is only then we can require society at large to adjust.

To all the Rahman's in the world, you are special… you are beautiful… you are precious and marvelous at God's sight. Don't be scared to release your inner self. Don't ever get to a point where you feel everyone is alike who are against you. Understand that for every bad situation that have come your way, divine creator has a plan and the plan is awesome, even when you can't see it yet.

THE AUTHOR

Abdul Rahman

Abdul Rahman is a 27-year-old musician, published poet, and an aspiring counselor. He loves to take photographs and make films whenever he has free time. More importantly, he loves Jesus! He loves spending time with animals, those battling mental illness, and family.

THE CO-AUTHOR

Dr. Princess Fumi S. Hancock, DNP, PMHNP-BC. CNP.

I AM THE PRINCESS OF SUBURBIA® LIVING IN DIASPORA as a Board Certified (PMHNP-BC) Psychiatric-Mental Health Dr. of Nurse Practice, YOUR COMPASSIONATE TRAUMA CARE MAESTRO™, Suicide Prevention & Child Rights Advocate, Your Life Rehab™ Ambassador.

She brings wealth and health to her audience by tackling mental wellness discussions such as depression, anxiety, suicide ideations, poor self-image, and other mental health disorders. She helps her clients use rehabilitative storytelling on their road to recovery. Dr. Hancock is the first African American to speak on Int'l. TEDx TALK Al Anjal National Schools platform in Saudi Arabia and the first woman recipient of the NAFCA African Oscar in Hollywood, California, and Indiefest Film Award Winner.

She is the host of her podcast, TEAR, the VEIL with Dr. Fumi, PsychDNP, hosted on several platforms such as iHeartRadio and iTunes. Dr. Princess Fumi Hancock is also the host of an Online Global Townhall show, Life RehabTV™.

Just recently, she was chosen as one of the very first Johnson and Johnson Nurse Innovation Fellow. She is the Founder & CEO of Pool of Bethesda Psychiatric Mental Health (POB Psychiatry).

More Information:
https://www.drfumipsychdnp.com/
https://www.pobpsychiatry.com/

What People Are Saying About Abdul Rahman

Everybody Needs Inspiration. Here is a little for Abdul Rahman:

"Abdul-Ramman,
I am thankful to Almighty Jehovah for your life, what a journey towards recovery, phew! May you forever be a channel of Light, Hope, and Victory in Jesus name, Amen"
Your Forever Mom!
-Adetutu Mojisola Diadem

"Abdul Rahman is an amazing writer with the ability to turn his life into a compelling journey to follow along. Tapping into the deepest emotions of the human experience, his raw and stylistic presence is one that's unforgettable"
-Razaaq Shittu

"Although he is a man of few words, Rahman carries an inspiring power in his voice. There is never a moment when his words are not intentional, uplifting, or speaking life in others."
-Zainab Shittu

"Beloved Rahman, may you continue to grow from strength to strength."
Love Always.
-*Aunty. Lara Ojebuoboh*

"A New Philosopher is Born
We are the grandparents of a new writer, a philosopher and an avid thinker. Ever since this prodigy was born into our family by our single-mother daughter, we did not realize that God blessed our family with this genius until he completed decided to continue his studies in Psychology. However, his interactions with us, his grandparents and with other siblings in his father's house clearly depict that his IQ is exceptionally high.
It is our pleasure to recommend this first work of Oluwadamilola Abdul Rahman, *Dami* for short, as a good writer to everyone eager to see how easy it is to develop raw psychology, after going through intrigues in a polygamous family."
-*Prince and Princess Theophilus and Eunice Ogunleye*